IT STARTED

WITH A PIE

SECRETS OF SWEET MAGNOLIA'S PIE LADY

WORDS MATTER
P U B L I S H I N G
OUR WORDS CHANGE THE WORLD

Words Matter Publishing
P.O. Box 1190
Decatur, IL 62525
www.wordsmatterpublishing.com

ISBN: 978-1-958000-95-3
Library of Congress Catalog Card Number: 2023946586

"I never was really a pie lover until I tried the delicious pies from Sweet Magnolia."

~ Gloria List

"The quality of all the goodies that we baked at Sweet Magnolia was amazing! The chocolate fudge cake was my very favorite!"

~Beth Dietrick

"The yeast rolls from Sweet Magnolia were absolutely wonderful! They melted in your mouth!"

~ Rick Moore

"I bought all my desserts from Sweet Magnolia and told everyone that I made them. I had to put my best foot forward. I simply could not confess my secret! I would pick my products up at the Shoppe's back door with no labels and in a brown paper bag!"

~ Anonymous

"The Triple Berry Pie was my favorite. Connie shared her recipe with me, and I make it quite often!"

~ Beth Ann Watson

"The chicken salad was the best! After Connie sold her business, I had to begin making it myself again!"

~ Jean Doyle

"We enjoyed Mimi's caramel cakes at the Don Moore Company picnics and many other company events! A southern taste that was indescribable! Sweet Magnolia's caramel cake was so moist and irresistible!"

~ Bob and Teri Meythaler

"My favorite part of every board meeting was when they brought in the Sweet Magnolia desserts!"

~ Mason Westerfield

"All the desserts were over the top! However, if I had to choose, the chicken salad was my favorite! I loved it in every way possible: on a sandwich, crackers, or fork! It disappeared way too fast in my fridge!"

~ Dede Foreman.

"A mom who turned humble pie into pure joy!"

~ Cathy Smith

"All of Sweet Magnolia's sweets are sinfully delicious, but my favorite was the Butterscotch Pie!"

~ Vicky Quisenberry

IT STARTED WITH A PIE

A collection of Recipes baked and tested in the Sweet
Magnolia Pie Shoppe in Lexington, Kentucky.

These oven temperatures and bake times were tested in
a Hobart convection oven.
Please adjust your oven temperatures and baking
times accordingly.

IN APPRECIATION AND WITH *love*

This cookbook is a compilation of my mother's recipes that she baked in her cake and pie shop, Sweet Magnolia, for 25 years. Our family has been blessed by her entrepreneurial spirit, grit, and dignity as she served the Lexington Area by offering her delicious and beautiful desserts. Our entire family has been spoiled by the high standard of desserts the Sweet Magnolia team baked under her direction.

During the last ten years after my mother retired from the pie business , our family has missed visiting the shoppe in Lexington and eating her delicious desserts. So we began talking about publishing a cookbook so our family could continue to bake and enjoy the Sweet Magnolia recipes. So I prodded and encouraged my mother to gather and send me all her recipes. Then, we whittled down the super sized recipes (with super size ingredient measurements) to: be used by any cook, at any age, in any well appointed kitchen. We especially wanted these recipes to be user friendly to inexperienced bakers and my young grandchildren who love to bake. My husband Don was invaluable as my preliminary editor, expert technology consultant, and critic. This family treasure is a love letter in honor of our Mother Connie. Publishing her delicious recipes will save and archive the Sweet Magnolia Recipes for our family to cherish for generations to come!

Thank you Mimi (Mee Mee) for passing on to us such a rich heritage of sacrifice, hard work, dedication, and determination! We all love you, and look forward to baking every one of these recipes during the holidays and every time we get a "sweet tooth". I love you very much! Marla

TABLE OF CONTENTS

COOKING RECIPES

THE PIE LADY

HOW DID YOU DECIDE TO START A PIE SHOPPE?

Well, that's a great question with a long story behind it. So let me tell you how this came to pass....

My early childhood memories are of the wonderful holidays I spent in Paintsville, Ky with my mother's family. As they arrived, we would unload all the homemade desserts and bread they brought for the Holiday meals. The dessert I got most excited about was my Aunt Dee Dee's homemade cream candy. My mother and her entire family were wonderful cooks. Thy took pride in every meal they made. My mother, later named Nana by my children, was the queen of her kitchen. Even Papa, my grandfather, made his own applesauce, apple butter, and churned butter. I loved eating his applesauce and sweet churned butter sandwiches. After lunch I would go sit in Papa's rocker on the front porch and fall asleep hunched over. My Aunt Dee Dee suggested I take Papa's belt and strap myself to the chair so I wouldn't fall out. So, I did!

I grew up on pies. My mother and father owned a drugstore in Pikeville, KY in 1947. My mother made all the pies to sell at the Soda Fountain. The seed was planted, but little did I know that I would one day own a Pie Shoppe.

Years passed, my children were grown, and I divorced. Immediately after the divorce, a friend asked if I would like to sell cars. Not having a lot of options in front of me, I decided to give it a try. For the next 8 years I worked in the Automobile business. Selling Cadillac, Mercedes, and BMW's, I found out the importance of taking care of the customer. More importantly, I learned how to sell and promote. This was a very important time in my life, and I really appreciated the confidence Joy Fairchild, the Dealer in Ashland Kentucky and others put in me.

After several years in the car-business I was getting a little restless. I took a well needed vacation and traveled to visit a girlfriend in California. While visiting, I was craving a piece of Banana or Coconut Cream pie. We spent the week eating pies in San Francisco, in search of the best Cream pie. After going to Marie Calendar's, Bakers Pies, Polly's Pies, and other franchises, I told my friend that I made better pies than any we had eaten!

On the plane home, I decided that I was going to give my entrepreneurial spirit a try and open my very own Pie Shoppe in Lexington, KY.

LIFE IS SHORT, EAT DESSERT FIRST   JACQUES TORRES

I did my research and found that at that time in Lexington, there was not a Pie Shoppe to be found. I began brainstorming names for my Pie Shoppe. My first choice was Mrs. Walden's Pie Shoppe (after my maiden name). Then I secured the Articles of Incorporation with the state and rented my first space on Southland Drive. After consulting with a sign maker, he informed me that the name I had chosen was too long to fit on the sign space. So, he suggested I call it Connie's Pies. But I told him that there was NO WAY I wanted my name on the sign in case the business failed. With time running out, as we stood in the parking lot in front of the space, we decided to call it Dottie's Pies (in honor of a lady who baked pies in Ashland).

The birth of Dottie's Pies was in August of 1989. In the beginning, we made 25 different cream and fruit pies. My success was immediate. But rather than traditional advertising, the week before opening, I delivered pies to everyone I had sold a BMW, Mercedes, Cadillac or Jaguar too! I also delivered pies to doctor's offices, lawyers offices and every professional business I could think of. After a few weeks of people sampling my pies, word spread fast and my pies were a hit!

Also, the Lexington McDonald's Franchise owner was a customer, and suggested that I place some of my pies at the Randall's Specialty Grocery store on Romany Road. The owner, Walt Barbour offered me a prime carousel as customers walked in the store. This brought a lot of attention to my desserts.

I delivered and sold 75-100 pieces of pie every week in Randall's. Shortly afterward, I also placed dessert carousels in the Pantry Fresh and Liquor Barn. I sold $89,000 dollars of pies that first year in those specialty locations. Our desserts were so tasty and beautiful that customers began to frequent the shoppe and many became weekly customers.

My son in law, Ross promoted the Pie Shoppe by delivering pies and gift certificates to his bank clients for Christmas! We also made beautiful boxes of Christmas cookies and bars that my children gave as gifts to beloved teachers and friends.

Six years later, my business was booming and I had outgrown the Southland space. Because our customers were requesting everything from cookies to cakes, even Wedding cakes, I began searching for a much larger space, and found a great location in Chinoe Center. I moved to this new location on September 5, 1995. I went from 1,000 square feet to 4,000 square feet. I had more than enough space and the sky was the limit for baking!

Before opening the new space, I decided that I also wanted a new name to go with my new location. After 6 years, I was tired of everyone calling me Dottie and explaining to them that it wasn't my name. So, I came up with the name Sweet Magnolia. From that point on, I was "The Pie Lady" of Sweet Magnolia".

Food

New shop offering 27 kinds of pies

CARROUT

Dottie's pies don't disappoint

First, you should know that I'm picky about pies.

I grew up surrounded by great pie-makers — with my grandmother leading the pack.

Chocolate meringue, lemon meringue, coconut cream, pecan, apple, cherry — you name it, someone in my family can make it.

Unfortunately, I didn't inherit the secret to producing creamy, perfect pies.

And now, thanks to Dottie, I don't have to worry about it.

When I first discovered Dottie's pies at Randall's on Romany Road, I was skeptical. Those big, fluffy pies couldn't possibly taste as good as they look.

But they do.

I've tried chocolate, lemon and butterscotch, and I haven't been disappointed once.

Other flavors include chess, pecan, cherry, banana cream, coconut, Keeneland Pie (chocolate chip and pecans) and apple.

There are two ways to get Dottie's pies. You can pick one up at Randall's on Romany Road or you can order directly from Dottie's Pie Shop, 270 Southland Drive, 277-2253. Most flavors are available for immediate pickup, but if you want to make sure they have your favorite, place your order a day ahead.

One drawback: The pies seem a little pricey. They sell for $9.95, except for cheesecake, which is $19.95.

But if you need a quick, delicious dessert for a dinner party or special occasion, it's money well spent. One pie easily serves eight.

— *Paula Anderson,
Lifestyle Editor*

Dottie's Pie Shop
Where: 270 Southland Drive
Phone: 277-2253
Pies are also available at Randall's on Romany Road.

FRUIT

Pies

Who doesn't love a good fruit pie? A fruit pie simply says southern hospitality.

There are many ways to eat a pie. Some dessert lovers stop at one piece; a la mode. Other connoisseurs must have two slices. My son in laws' father, Don Jr., would just stand in the kitchen and eat one or two bites at a time right out of the pie plate until the triple berry pie was gone. Grandaddy Walden could eat half a pie after dinner and never gain a pound.

**If pie is your "thing" as it is mine, I'm sure you will find
a new favorite one in this collection!**

10

Sweet Magnolia Flaky Pie Crust

A flaky pie crust is the most important foundation for any delicious pie. Without a perfect pie crust, your pie will not be as scrumptious! In fact, it is hard to buy a really tasty pie crust. A homemade crust is always best and worth the extra time and effort. It is possible to save time by freezing the rolled, plated, and tightly covered crusts ahead of time. Then, you will be ready to use a perfect flaky crust at any time.

INGREDIENTS

2 cups of Hudson"s Cream all-purpose flour or an all-purpose white baking flour of your choice. (like King Arthur's)
½ tsp. salt
1 ½ sticks of cold, diced small pieces of butter
3 Tbsps. butter flavored solid Crisco shortening
¼ cup of ice water

DIRECTIONS

1. In a bowl, combine flour and salt and set aside. Add butter to a mixing bowl. Blend in the flour and salt with the whisk. Then add the shortening and continue to blend until mixture resembles course meal.

2. At this point, use your paddle accessory if you have one. Turn the mixer on low and sprinkle Ice water over the mixture evenly. Blend mixture well until all is moistened and forms a dough consistency. Turn mixer on high and blend for ten more seconds.

3. Gather pastry and press together until it can be formed into an oblong rectangle (about 4"x6"). Wrap in plastic wrap or put in a baggie. Place in refrigerator for at least one hour. The dough will stay fresh in the refrigerator for weeks. The dough can also be frozen for months before using.

4. When ready to use the dough, remove from the refrigerator and let set out 30 minutes before rolling out. The dough should remain chilly to roll out easily.

5. Sprinkle board or table with flour. Flour both sides of the pastry. Place flattened flour rectangle on board or table and begin to roll out, starting in the center and rolling to the edge in one direction. Turn the pastry ¼ around as you roll out to keep pastry from sticking to table. Pastry should be a 13"-14" round circle for a 10" pie pan. Do not grease the pie pan!!!

6. Fold pastry circle in half so you can lift it into pie pan. Place fold in center of Pie Plate and unfold pastry. Pick up the pie plate and drop gently on counter-top a few times until pie crust settles in the plate. Take your finger and gently press around the edge of the bottom of the pie crust.

7. Trim the large Pastry around the pie plate so the edges of pie crust are ¾" hanging over the pie plate.

8. Turn the edges under and roll edges under to make it lie thick and even around the top of the pie pan. Also, make sure the crust is stuck tight to the sides of pan and around the outside top so the crust does not shrink into the pie pan. Then, pinch all around the edge of the pastry until beautiful. Now, gently press all around the sides and up the sides of the pie crust to eliminate any pie shrinkage.

9. Set crust aside until you are ready to pour in the filling, or cover well with plastic wrap and place in the freezer to use later.

LIFE IS SHORT, EAT DESSERT FIRST   JACQUES TORRES

Triple Berry Pie

This is one of our customers' favorite berry pies. The second-best way to eat a Tripleberry Pie is to turn the pie over on a platter, gently stir, and serve with ice cream as a cobbler!

INGREDIENTS

One unbaked pie crust (see recipe page 12)
One rolled-out pie pastry for the top crust of the pie.

1 cup all-purpose flour
1 cup dark brown sugar
1 cup white granulated sugar
2 T tapioca
1/8 tsp salt
1/2 stick butter (diced in small pieces)
1 T lemon juice
30 ounces of fruit (frozen fruit sets up better!!!)
(10 oz. of Each fruit: Seedless Blackberries, Blueberries and Raspberries)

DIRECTIONS

1. Preheat oven to 325°.
2. Combine all dry ingredients in a small bowl.
3. Place fresh or frozen fruit in a large bowl and sprinkle with lemon juice. Pour dry mix over fruit and toss gently.
4. Pour fruit mixture in a pie shell and mound in the center. Evenly spread remaining dry mix over the pie.
5. Place diced butter evenly around top of fruit.
6. Top with rolled out pastry and pinch edges of pastries together. Make 2" slits in top pastry so fruit can breathe.
7. Lightly brush top pastry with an egg wash (one egg white). Lightly Sprinkle pastry with Sugar.
8. Place pie in oven on middle rack and bake for at least 50-60 minutes or until inside of fruit mixture bubbles up. Once pie bubbles, cook for another 3-5 minutes until golden brown.
9. Take out of oven and cool on rack.

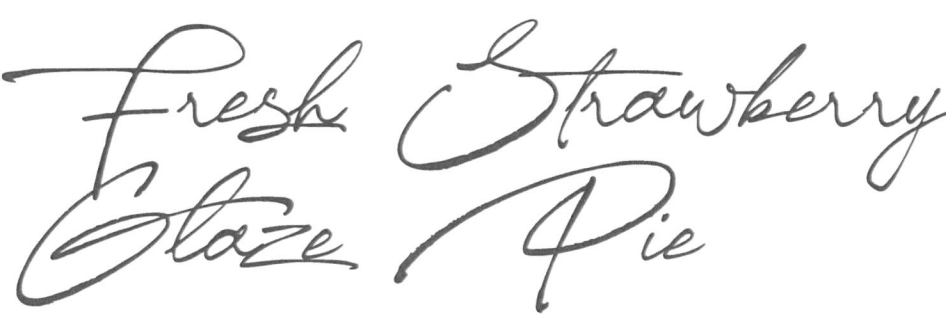
Fresh Strawberry Glaze Pie

This is a wonderful summer dessert that should be made with ripe fresh strawberries – preferably from the farmers market!

INGREDIENTS

1 10" BAKED and perforated pie shell
(see recipe page 12)

5 cups water

2 ¾ cups sugar

1 cup plus 1 Tbsp. strawberry Jello

1-2 drops red food coloring

¾ cup corn starch

1-2 quarts of fresh red ripe whole
Strawberries - washed, topped, and dried

DIRECTIONS

1. Combine and stir sugar and corn starch in a small bowl.
2. Add water, Jello, red food coloring and corn starch/sugar mixture to saucepan.
3. Stir glaze on medium heat using a flat edged spoon held on the bottom of the pan. Stir constantly until thick. Bring to boil and stir vigorously and constantly for 5 minutes. Cool.
4. Place whole strawberries (point up) in a baked and perforated pie Shell. Then half about ½ cup of berries and place in between whole berries to fill in the gaps.
5. Pour cool glaze over the strawberries. Place in the refrigerator to chill. This pie will keep fresh for 2 weeks.
6. Serve with fresh whipped cream.

Blueberry Pie

INGREDIENTS

One unbaked pie crust (See recipe on page 12)
One rolled-out pie pastry for the top crust
of the pie.

1 cup all-purpose flour

1 cup dark brown sugar

1 cup white granulated sugar

2 T tapioca

1/8 tsp salt

1/2 stick butter (diced in small pieces)

1 T lemon juice

30 ounces of blueberries (frozen fruit sets up better!!!)

DIRECTIONS

1. Preheat oven to 325°.
2. Combine all dry ingredients in a small bowl.
3. Place fresh or frozen fruit in a large bowl and sprinkle with lemon juice. Pour dry mix over fruit and toss gently.
4. Pour fruit mixture in a pie shell and mound in the center. Evenly spread remaining Dry Mix over the pie.
5. Place diced butter evenly around top of fruit.
6. Top with rolled pastry and pinch edges of pastries together. Make 2" slits in top pastry so fruit can breathe.
7. Lightly brush top pastry with an egg wash (one egg beaten). Lightly Sprinkle pastry with Sugar.
8. Place pie in oven on middle rack and bake for at least 50-60 minutes or until inside of fruit mixture bubbles up. Once pie bubbles, cook for another 3-5 minutes until golden brown.
9. Take out of oven and allow to cool on rack.

Bumbleberry Pie

This fruit pie is a smorgasbord of every fruit in your refrigerator or farmer's market. It was not quite as popular as our Tripleberry pie for some reason. However, both berry pies are full of flavor and tasty fruit goodness!

INGREDIENTS

One unbaked pie crust (See recipe on page 12)
One rolled-out pie pastry for the top crust of the pie.
1 cup all-purpose flour
1 cup dark brown sugar
1 cup white granulated sugar
2 T tapioca
1/8 tsp salt
1/2 stick butter (diced in small pieces)
1 T lemon juice
30 ounces of fruit (frozen fruit sets up better!!!)
(6oz. of Each fruit: Seedless Blackberries, Blueberries and Raspberries)

DIRECTIONS

1. Preheat oven to 325°.
2. Combine all dry ingredients in a small bowl.
3. Place fresh or frozen fruit in a large bowl and sprinkle with lemon juice. Pour dry mix over fruit and toss gently.
4. Pour fruit mixture in a pie shell and mound in the center. Evenly spread remaining dry mix over the pie.
5. Place diced butter evenly around top of fruit.
6. Top with rolled pastry and pinch edges of pastries together. Make 2" slits in top pastry so fruit can breathe.
7. Lightly brush top pastry with an egg wash (one egg beaten). Lightly sprinkle pastry with sugar.
8. Place pie in oven on middle rack and bake for at least 50-60 minutes or until inside of fruit mixture bubbles up. Once pie bubbles, cook for another 3-5 minutes until golden brown.

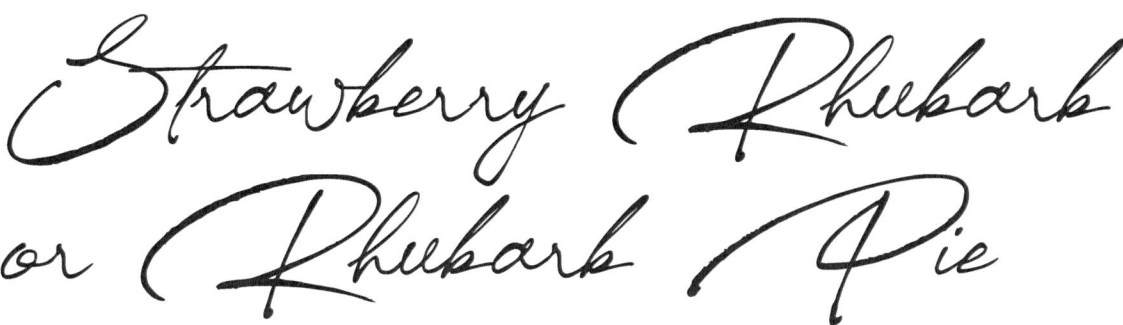

Strawberry Rhubarb or Rhubarb Pie

In 1989 when I began my pie business, you could not even buy a rhubarb pie anywhere. In fact, pies were not even in vogue. My Aunt Dee Dee made the first rhubarb pie for me, and I loved it! I introduced rhubarb pie to our menu only at the request.

INGREDIENTS

One unbaked pie crust (See recipe on page 12)
One rolled-out pie pastry for the top crust of the pie.

1 cup all-purpose flour
1 cup dark brown sugar
1 cup white granulated sugar
2 T tapioca
1/8 tsp salt
1/2 stick butter (diced in small pieces)
1 T lemon juice
30 ounces of fruit (frozen fruit sets up better!!!)
(15 oz Rhubarb and 15 oz strawberries)

DIRECTIONS

1. Preheat oven to 325°.
2. Combine all dry ingredients in a small bowl.
3. Place fresh or frozen fruit in a large bowl and sprinkle with lemon juice. Pour dry mix over fruit and toss gently.
4. Pour fruit mixture in a pie shell and mound fruit in the center. Evenly spread remaining dry mix over the pie.
5. Place diced butter evenly around top of fruit.
6. Top with rolled pastry and pinch edges of pastries together. Make 2" slits in top pastry so fruit can breathe.
7. Lightly brush top pastry with an egg wash (one egg beaten). Lightly sprinkle pastry with sugar.
8. Place in oven on middle rack and bake for at least 50-60 minutes or until inside of fruit mixture bubbles up. Once pie bubbles, cook for another 3-5 minutes until golden brown.

CREAM
Pies

Our family has always enjoyed pies! During my childhood, we never ate cake: only pie. I never actually saw my mother nor my grandmother make a cake. My family only ate pie for dessert!

My parents owned a drug store in Pikeville, Kentucky, and my mother (or Nana) made all the pies for the soda fountain. Butterscotch Cream Pie was everyone's favorite! Although my father, Dr. Walden, would eat any pie offered him!

I never even tried making a pie until I became interested in starting my pie business in August 1989. However, I had curiously observed and stored in my memory, my mother and grandmother making many pies as I walked through our kitchen. So starting a pie business for me was no problem!

When I started my pie business in Southland Shopping center in Lexington, we made all the wonderful pies that I grew up enjoying plus many other varieties! We made 31 types of pies in my 900 square foot kitchen. We soon outgrew this kitchen in five years.

After six successful months of business, customers began to ask if we were going to make cakes and other goodies. I realized that to grow my business I would need to offer many more selections. At the time, I did not have room for commercial ovens, so I began with baking pound cakes. Soon after, we added cheese cakes to the dessert offering. I ended up adding over 56 other desserts, lunch bites and snacks. Therefore, I found a new 4000 square foot space in Chinoe Shopping Center. We remained in that location for 18 more years, 25 years total.

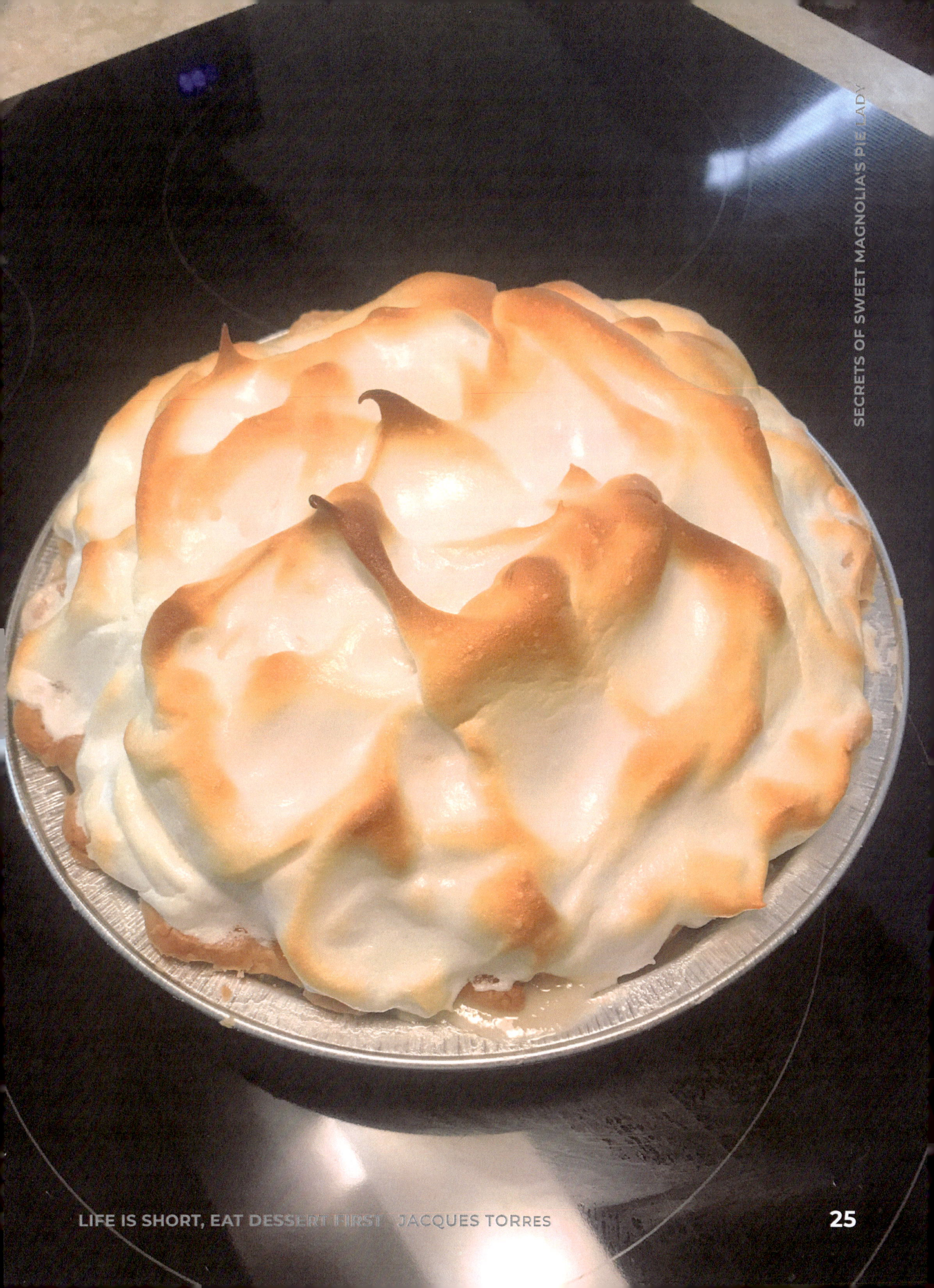

Meringue Topping

We were fortunate that in our baking industry, we could purchase an egg stabilizer that kept our beautiful Sweet Magnolia 3" high meringues fresh and stable for two weeks. You can't buy this product in the grocery stores anymore. However, in our family, most pies will not last two days anyway so the meringue does not need to stay fresh for very long!

INGREDIENTS

4 large egg whites (room temperature)
2 tsp. cream of tarter
6 Tbsps. very fine granulated sugar
½ tsp. of vanilla

DIRECTIONS

Cool Pies Before Adding Meringue

1. Preheat oven to 325°.
2. Separate egg whites from egg yolks in two small perfectly clean bowls making sure to remove any sperm from egg white with a spoon.
3. Let egg whites become room temperature before beating or peaks will not form well.
4. Beat the egg whites on the highest speed on mixer until firm peaks have formed.
5. Add the vanilla and continue to beat until blended.
6. Add the cream of tarter and mix well.
7. Gradually, fold in super fine sugar, one Tbsp. at a time until all is combined in whites. Continue beating until stiff peaks form.
8. Pile meringue on top of pre-baked pie. Be careful to seal the meringue onto the edge of pie crust to prevent shrinkage.
9. Place about 4" under the heat and bake about 10-12 minutes, until golden. Cool completely.

Coconut Cream Pie

Before I opened my pie shop, I was visiting my girlfriend Elaina in San Francisco. Every day, for one week, we searched for a new pie shop and ate a piece of coconut cream pie to determine who made the most delicious pies in San Francisco. At the end of that week, I decided that I made better pies than any we had tasted. So, I told Elaina that I was going to go home and open-up a pie shop in Lexington!

INGREDIENTS

1 pre-baked pie crust (see recipe page 12)
5 Tbsps. plus 1 tsp. packed corn starch
2 cups sugar
½ tsp. salt
4 eggs separated
2 ½ cups whole milk
3 Tbsps. butter
2 ¾ tsps. Vanilla
⅓ cup water
1 ¾ cup coconut

DIRECTIONS

1. Allow eggs to sit out of refrigerator until they become room temperature.
2. Separate egg yolks from egg whites (save egg whites for meringue).
3. In another small bowl, add the corn starch and sugar and mix up.
4. In a blender, add egg yolks, salt, water, vanilla and sugar mixture. Whip.
5. Put milk and only ¾ cup of coconut, in a 3-quart saucepan and heat until it steams and froths, stirring constantly.
6. Take ⅓ cup of the heated mixture and add to the blender and Whip. Pour all the blended mixture back into the saucepan.
7. Stir constantly with a flat edged spoon, bring this mixture in the saucepan to a full boil. Boil for 2 minutes, stirring vigorously with a flat edged spoon to prevent sticking. (you may want to use a hand mixer this last 2 minutes*).
8. Remove saucepan from heat and add 3 butter. Stir briskly until butter melts.
9. Remove saucepan from heat and allow to cool for 5 minutes.
10. Toast the remaining 1 cup of coconut. Allow it to cool and then cover the pudding pie with coconut. Top pie with a Meringue (See recipe page 26). Sprinkle toasted coconut over meringue.

Chocolate Cream Pie

This dessert is absolutely a chocolate lovers delight! It was the most popular cream pie we sold! We made 30 cream pies on Monday of every week. We were constantly stirring off cream pies to replenish daily our stock of 30 fresh cream pies. There is no doubt that cream pies are the most difficult pies to perfect! But this delicious pie is worth the effort and challenge!

INGREDIENTS

1 pre-baked 10" pie crust (see recipe page 12)
5 Tbsps. plus 1 tsp. packed corn starch
2 cup sugar
½ tsp. salt
4 eggs - separated
2 ½ cups milk
3 Tbsps. butter
2 ¾ tsps. vanilla
⅓ cup of water
½ cup of cocoa

DIRECTIONS

1. Separate room temperature egg yolks from egg whites (save whites for meringue topping).
2. Combine the corn starch and sugar in a small bowl and set aside. (so the corn starch will dissolve easily).
3. In a 2 ½ - quart saucepan, heat the milk and 1 Tbsp. butter until it steams and froths, stirring constantly with a flat edge spoon. Keep the flat edge spoon on the bottom of the pan at all times while you stir constantly.
4. Put the egg yolks, cocoa, salt, water, vanilla and sugar mixture in a blender and whip ten seconds.
5. Remove from heat and set aside.
6. Take ⅓ cup of heated mixture and add to the blender. Blend a few seconds.
7. Pour all blended mixture into the saucepan. Heat and stir briskly and constantly until it comes to a full boil. Boil for 2 minutes; whipping vigorously and constantly to prevent sticking. "Whip it Good!"
8. Remove saucepan from heat and add 2 Tbsps. of butter and stir briskly until butter melts .
9. Pour the pudding mixture into the bottom of the pie shell. Top with meringue (Recipe on page 26).
10. When cutting your meringue pie, use a large smooth-edged knife. Dip the knife in water every time you cut a slice in your pie.

Luau Cream Pie

This is a tasty and refreshing summer dessert and makes you feel like you are indulging on an Island in Hawaii!

INGREDIENTS

1 pre-baked pie crust (see recipe page 12)

4 Tbsps. of corn starch

1 cup of sugar

½ cup of shredded coconut

½ can of water

4 eggs - yolks separated from whites

1 tsps. vanilla

Firm fresh bananas

1 can (8 oz.) of sweetened crushed pineapple with juice

DIRECTIONS

1. Separate egg yolks from egg whites (save whites for meringue topping) and whip 4 egg yolks.

2. Combine the corn starch and sugar in a small bowl and set aside. (in order for the corn starch to dissolve easily).

3. In a 3-quart saucepan: Combine coconut, drained pineapple, and water.

4. Heat until it steams and froths, stirring constantly. Then add corn starch, vanilla extract and sugar mixture, stirring constantly.

5. Remove from heat and set aside.

6. Take ⅓ cup of heated mixture and add to the 4 whipped egg yolks; stirring constantly. Return all egg mixture to saucepan. You will know that the mixture is ready to boil when the frothing has disappeared.

7. Boil for 2 minutes; stirring vigorously to prevent sticking.

8. Remove from heat and add 3 Tbsps. of margarine. Mix well until melted.

9. Pour a cup of pudding mixture into the bottom of the pie shell. Important: Let this cool for ten minutes. THEN, after mixture is cool, cover the pudding completely with firm fresh sliced Bananas. (start on the outside and make a circle. Let bananas overlap in a circle).

10. Cover the bananas with remaining pudding, refrigerate and cool before topping with meringue. (See recipe page 26)

Butterscotch Cream Pie

Most young people today have never tried a Butterscotch pie. It is a very delicious pie that most who try it, love it! I opened the first retail pie shop in Lexington, Kentucky. Our Butterscotch pie became a very popular dessert. Sweet Magnolia Pie Shop sold our cream pies to a few local restaurants for their dessert menus.

INGREDIENTS

1 pre-baked pie crust (see recipe page 12)

2 ½ cups of whole milk

3 Tbsps. butter

⅓ cup of Water

3 Tbsp. of maple flavoring

5 Tbsps. - plus 1 tsp. of corn starch, packed tightly

1 ½ cup of dark brown sugar, packed tightly

4 eggs, room temperature and separated.

NOTE: Save whites for meringue

DIRECTIONS

1. In a small bowl , stir together the brown sugar and corn starch. Set aside.

2. Pour 4 egg yolks, water, maple flavoring, corn starch, brown sugar mixture, and salt, into a blender. Blend for 10 seconds (This is a heavy mixture so blender may labor a bit) Set this aside.

3. Pour the milk and 1 Tbsp. of butter into a 3-quart pan.

4. Stir on medium high heat with a flat top edge spoon until steamy, set aside

5. Pour only 1 cup of this hot mixture into the blender and mix a few seconds.

6. Pour the blender mixture into the steamy milk, stirring constantly back and forth, keeping the mixture from sticking. Keep the flat edge of your spoon on the bottom of pan at all times. Bring to a boil and whip vigorously for 2 minutes until thickened.

7. When thickened like pudding, remove from heat and add 2 Tbsps. of butter. Whip thoroughly until butter is melted and stirred in.

8. Cool and stir occasionally for a couple of minutes. This will make sure that you don't get a film on top of the mixture. Pour into a baked pie shell. Cool to room temperature, and then top with meringue (see recipe page 26).

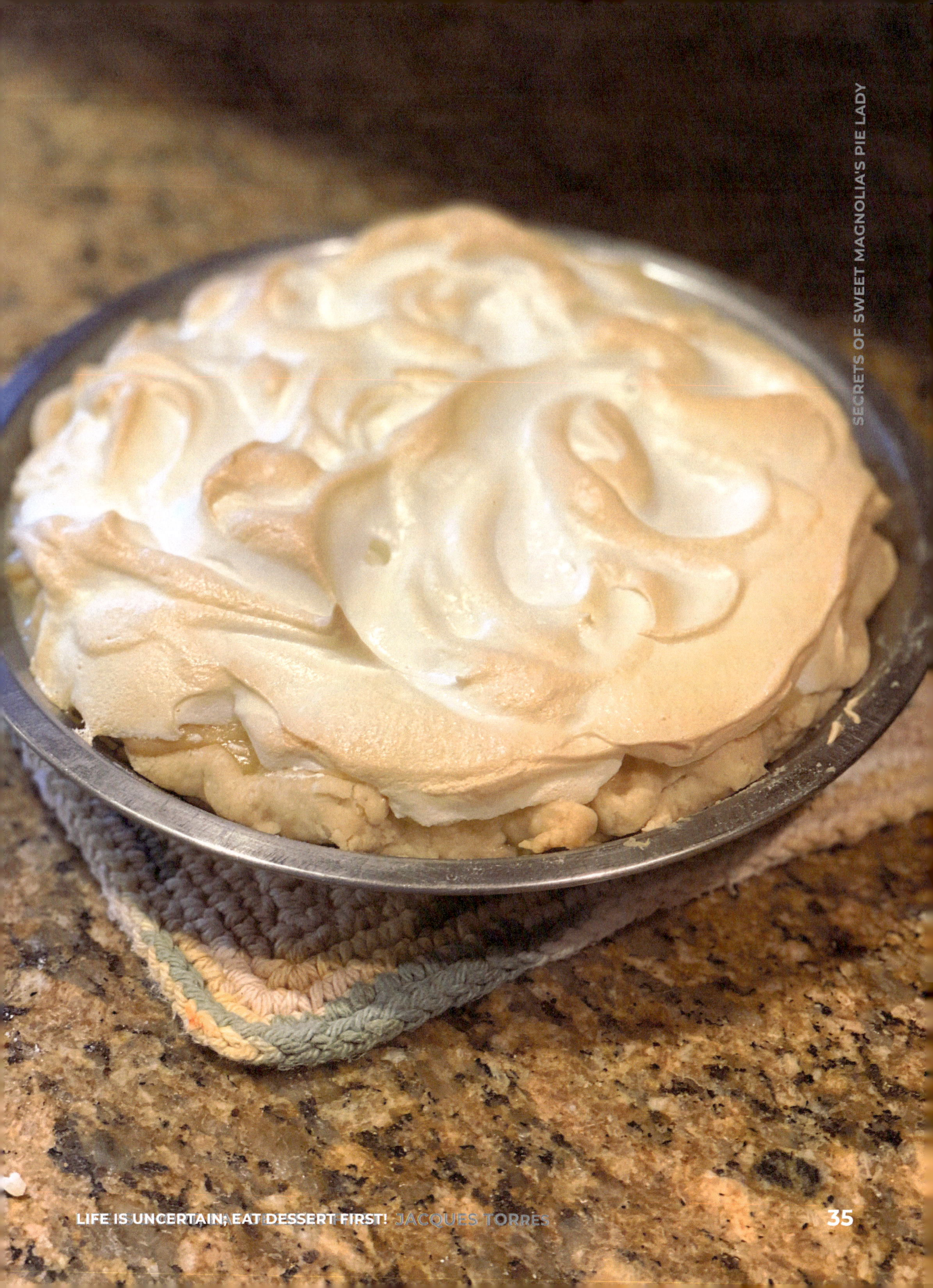

Banana Cream Pie

Banana Cream Pie is banana pudding in a pie! If you prefer, you can leave off the meringue, add fresh whipped cream, and serve delicious banana pudding!

INGREDIENTS

1 pre-baked pie crust (see recipe page 12)
5 Tbsps. plus 1 tsp. packed corn starch
2 cups sugar
½ tsp. salt
4 eggs - separated
2 ½ cups milk
3 Tbsps. butter
2 ¾ tsps. vanilla
⅓ cup of water
Fresh firm bananas

DIRECTIONS

1. Separate room temperature egg yolks from egg whites (save whites for meringue topping).
2. Combine the corn starch and sugar in a small bowl and set aside. (so the corn starch will dissolve easily).
3. Put the egg yolks, salt, water, vanilla and sugar mixture in a blender and whip ten seconds.
4. In a 3-quart saucepan, heat the milk and 1 Tbsp. butter until it steams and froths, stirring constantly.
5. Remove from heat and set aside.
6. Take ⅓ cup of heated mixture and add to the blender. Blend a few seconds.
7. Pour all blended mixture into the saucepan. Heat and stir briskly and constantly until it comes to a full boil. Boil for 2 minutes; stirring constantly to prevent sticking.
8. Remove saucepan from heat and add 2 Tbsps. of butter and stir briskly until butter melts.
9. Pour a cup of pudding mixture into the bottom of the pie shell. Important: Let this cool for 5 minutes. Cover the pudding completely with firm fresh sliced bananas. (start on the outside and make a circle. Let bananas overlap in a circle).
10. Cover the bananas with the remaining of the pudding and cool before topping with meringue (see recipe page 26).

Baked Egg Custard Pie

This creamy dessert is Cream Brûlée in a pie shell! If you bake and refrigerate, it is heaven, a little slice at a time!

INGREDIENTS

1 pre-baked pie crust (see recipe page 12)
2 ⅓ cups whole milk
4 large eggs
¾ cup sugar
½ tsp. salt
1 tsp. vanilla

DIRECTIONS

1. In bowl, whip by hand 4 large eggs.
2. Add the sugar, salt and vanilla to eggs and whip by hand. Strain mixture through a strainer into a bowl.
3. In a saucepan, heat milk to scalding. (Scalded milk forms tiny bubbles around the edges of the pan, and steam rises from the milk.)
4. On low speed, pour warm milk mixture into eggs gradually.
5. Pour filling into one 10" pie crust.
6. Place pie in a 325° preheated oven on BOTTOM RACK! Bake pie for 45 minutes. Turn oven off and keep the door closed. Leave in oven an additional 7-10 minutes. Take out of oven and sprinkle with nutmeg.

* To make a coconut custard pie: add ½ cup coconut to egg mixture before baking.

Lemon Meringue Pie

Lemon Meringue pie is a delightful summer favorite. Fresh squeezed lemon juice gives the pie its zest and makes you dream of a summer day!

This cream pie is also very delicious topped with cool whip instead of meringue.

INGREDIENTS

1 pre-baked pie crust (see recipe page 12)
5 Tbsps. of corn starch
1 ½ cup of sugar
3 Tbsps. of butter
⅓ cup of lemon juice
2 cups of warm water
4 eggs - room temperature
(Separate the yolks from the egg whites)
NOTE: Save whites for meringue

DIRECTIONS

1. Separate egg yolks from egg whites (save whites for Meringue topping) and whip egg yolks.
2. Combine the corn starch and sugar in a small bowl and set aside. (so the corn starch will dissolve easily).
3. In a 3-quart saucepan, combine the lemon juice and water. Heat until it steams and froths, stirring constantly.
4. Then add corn starch and sugar mixture, stirring constantly.
5. Remove from heat and set aside.
6. Take ⅓ cup of heated mixture and add to the 4 whipped egg yolks; stirring briskly so eggs will not cook early.
7. Return all egg mixture to saucepan. Again, stir briskly and constantly with a flat edge spoon until it comes to a full boil. Boil for 2 minutes; stirring constantly to prevent sticking.
8. Remove saucepan from heat and add 3 Tbsps. of butter and stir briskly until butter melts .
9. Pour the pudding mixture into the bottom of the pre-baked pie shell. Important: Let this cool for ten minutes.
10. Cover the pie with fresh Meringue (see recipe page 26) and bake meringue.
11. Cool before serving. Store in refrigerator.

SWEET

Pies

When I think of dessert, pies are what comes to my mind! Making a delicious pie is much more trouble than a cake. Therefore, most bakers make cakes or cookies. You can't have a tasty pie without a homemade flaky pie crust! It is one more step before you can begin to craft any pie.

Until I opened my first pie shop, I did not realize how few people really know how to bake a yummy sweet pie. I hope this cookbook will inspire others to learn the "art" of the PIE!

My employees cutting and preparing "sampler pies"

 Pecan Pie

Very few families celebrate Thanksgiving without a pumpkin and pecan pie. These two desserts are so very easy for any novice baker.

INGREDIENTS

1 unbaked fresh pie crust that you prepare and freeze ahead. (this prevents shrinkage) (see recipe page 12)

5 eggs
1 cup of brown sugar
¼ cup of white sugar
2 Tbsps. flour
1 Tbsp. vanilla
¼ tsp. salt
½ cup dark Karo Syrup
¼ cup melted butter
½ cup light Karo Syrup or maple syrup
1 ¼ cup of pecan pieces

DIRECTIONS

1. *Preheat oven to 425°. Use a frozen pie crust.*
2. *Wrap edges of pie shell with a strip of aluminum foil: crimped around edges of crust.*
3. *Layer pecans in the bottom of the unbaked pie crust evenly.*
4. *Mix Eggs and sugar in a mixer on low to break and blend. Only blend for 30 seconds. Blending longer will cause foam to appear. Excess foam can be removed with a spoon, skimming the top lightly.*
5. *Add the vanilla and salt and stir in just long enough to blend.*
6. *Add Karo syrups and blend.*
7. *Pour all mixture into the pie shell. Pecans will rise slowly to the top.*
8. *Bake for 10 minutes at 425°.*
9. *Reduce heat to 350° and bake for 25-35 minutes plus until center of pie gels. If pecans get too brown before center has gelled, cover with a disposable pie tin.*

Fudgie Peanut Butter Pie

This Pie recipe is very rich and decadent! It was one of my customers very favorites that was included in our sampler pie offering. Our Sampler pies contained 10 slices of 5 different pies. In one sampler pie , which I sold for $25 , the customer received two slices each of Pecan, Chess, Fudgy Peanut Butter, Keenland, and Brownie pie! It was a very popular pie selection because it was possible to enjoy five different pies for one price! It was truly the best holiday gift! Hundreds of these pies were given away by regular customers to their clients and employees during the holidays!

A)PREPARING THE CRUST

INGREDIENTS

10" flaky pie crust (see recipe page 12)
2 cups dried beans or ceramic baking beads or weights
1 - 10" wax paper circle

DIRECTIONS

1. Preheat Oven to 325°
2. Line crust with the wax paper circle and spread 2 cups dried beans around top of paper touching the sides of pie shell.
3. Place pie shell in oven and bake for 20 minutes. Then remove and cool. Remove beans and circle out of pie shell.

B) CARMEL PECAN FILLING

INGREDIENTS

¾ stick butter
1 cup honey
¾ cup dark brown sugar
¼ cup whipping cream
1 cup pecan pieces

DIRECTIONS

1. Preheat oven to 350°.
2. Put the butter, honey, and dark brown sugar in a saucepan.
3. Cook on low and stir until butter melts.
4. Turn on medium high and stir constantly. Bring to a boil and boil for one minute.
5. Take pan off burner and quickly stir in heavy whipping cream.
6. Place pecans in bottom of pre-baked pie shell then pour sauce over them.
7. Place in oven and bake for 10- 15 minutes until it bubbles.
8. Remove from oven and let cool.

C) PEANUT BUTTER TOPPING

DIRECTIONS

Combine 1 cup of peanut butter and ¾ cup powdered sugar. Spread on top of caramel filling.

D) CHOCOLATE TOPPING

DIRECTIONS

1. Melt 1 ½ cup semi-sweet chocolate chips in a double boiler. Add ¼ cup whipping cream. Pour over peanut butter topping.

LIFE IS SHORT, EAT DESSERT FIRST   JACQUES TORRES

Old Fashioned Transparent Pie

This recipe was handed down to me from my mother- in law, Myrtle Minix. She always served this sweet pie when we celebrated the holidays at her home in Paintsville, Kentucky.

INGREDIENTS

¾ cup of half and half cream

1 Tbsp. of vanilla

1 - 10" pie crust, unbaked, no perforations (see recipe page 12)

1 cup light brown sugar

¼ cup of red currant jelly (or grape)

¾ Stick of room temperature butter

3 level Tbsps. of corn starch

3 eggs separated (use egg yolks - save whites for meringue if desired)

DIRECTIONS

1. Preheat oven to 325°.
2. Combine sugar and corn starch in a small bowl.
3. Add the mixture to the butter and cream together on low speed.
4. Add the beaten egg yolks.
5. Add vanilla.
6. Stir in cream, then mix well.
7. Spread the jelly lightly over the bottom of the unbaked pie shell.
8. Pour the filling over the current jelly.
9. Bake until the mixture thickens at 325° for 40-45 minutes or until golden brown on the middle rack of oven .

German Chocolate Pie

INGREDIENTS

1 pie crust (see recipe page 12)

½ stick of butter

2 large eggs

1 ½ cups of sugar

3 Tbsps. of corn starch

⅛ tsp. salt

1 tsp. of vanilla

1 ¼ cup of coconut

1 (12 oz.) can of evaporated milk

½ cup of chopped pecans

1 (4 oz.) block of bakers German
chocolate squares

DIRECTIONS

1. Preheat oven to 325°.
2. Melt in a small saucepan: German's chocolate and ½ stick of butter.
3. In a mixing bowl, combine eggs, sugar, corn starch, salt and vanilla.
4. Combine chocolate mixture and egg mixture.
5. Add: 1 can of evaporated milk and mix well.
6. Pour into 1 pie crust shell.
7. Top pie with ¼ cup of coconut and ½ cup of chopped pecans.
8. Using the handle end of a fork or spoon, gently submerge coconut and pecans into the chocolate mixture at least 8 times.
9. Bake for approximately 45 minutes depending on your oven. (check after 30 minutes to see if the pies are baking evenly. Rotate pies if unevenly browned. Cover with a tent of aluminum foil if crust is too brown
10. The top of the pie should be crusty and firm. Always check the middle by gently touching with your fingertips. It should feel solid and firm.

Chess Pie

A Chess Pie is the pie of the ages! It has never gone out of style because of the simplicity of ingredients, it is still a delicious and savory dessert that most people like.

INGREDIENTS

½ cup butter

1 ¾ cups sugar

4 whole eggs - room temperature

2 ½ Tbsps. vinegar

½ tsp. vanilla (optional)

⅛ tsp. salt

1 - 10" unbaked pie shell (see recipe page 12)

(use a frozen pie shell -this prevents shrinkage)

DIRECTIONS

1. *Preheat oven to 325°.*
2. *Place room temperature eggs in an electric mixer and beat on low.*
3. *Add sugar all at once and continue to blend.*
4. *Strain egg mixture back to mixing bowl.*
5. *Add vinegar, vanilla, and salt. Mix well.*
6. *Add melted butter and blend.*
7. *Pour into the unbaked pie crust.*
8. *Bake at 325° on BOTTOM RACK for 45-50 minutes until firm. Turn oven off and leave the door closed for 10 more minutes. Take out of the oven.*

Keenland Pie

This was Sweet Magnolia's version of a Derby or May Day Pie. We coined the name Keenland Pie after the local thoroughbred horse race track in Lexington Kentucky. This pie is a traditional Kentucky Derby Day favorite!

INGREDIENTS

1 pie crust (see recipe page 12)

6 eggs

6 oz. of dark brown sugar

1 Tbsp. vanilla

2 Tbsps. bourbon

¾ cup sugar

2 Tbsps. flour

9 oz. corn syrup

6 Tbsps. melted butter

¼ cup walnuts

¼ cup pecans

½ cup chocolate chips

DIRECTIONS

1. Preheat Oven to 350°.
2. Blend the eggs on low speed.
3. Add the sugars, vanilla, bourbon and flour into the egg mixture and blend.
4. Add the corn syrup and melted butter and blend. (If corn syrup is too thick to pour out of bottle, place bottle in hot water to make it easier to pour)
5. Layer the chocolate chips and then nuts evenly on the bottom of pie shell.
6. Pour liquid mixture over the nuts and chips.
7. Place pie in oven and bake 50 -60 minutes, until gelled. If pie gets too brown cover with a pie tin or piece of aluminum foil.

Brownie Pie

The smell of baking brownies, in general, just makes your mouth water! Therefore, this pie was a crowd pleaser! For an added touch, you can serve this pie with ice cream and caramel sauce drizzled over it. In addition, if you bake this pie right before your guests arrive for a dinner party, they will never forget what a great hostess you are!

A) PREPARING THE CRUST

INGREDIENTS

2 sticks of butter: softened

¼ cup flour

2 ⅓ cup sugar

7 cups of walnuts (ground in blender)

DIRECTIONS

1. Mix first three ingredients.
2. Then mix in walnuts.
3. Place this crust mixture in refrigerator to firm up.
4. Mold 2 cups of crust mixture on sides of a pie plate.
5. Add remaining amount of mixture to bottom of pie plate and contour the crust into the pie plate. Build up the edge of pie crust around edge of pie plate to form a thick border to pie. Freeze this crust until ready to use.

B) BROWNIE FILLING

INGREDIENTS

2 sticks butter

2 cups sugar

4 eggs

4 oz. of semi-sweet chocolate slightly softened in microwave

⅛ tsp. salt

½ cup flour

2 tsps. vanilla

1 cup walnut pieces

DIRECTIONS

1. Preheat Oven to 325°.
2. Cream together the butter and sugar in a mixer.
3. Add eggs.
4. Add remaining ingredients, except walnuts, and blend.
5. Pour mixture in your frozen crust and smooth evenly. Sprinkle a few more Walnut pieces on top to bake attractively.
6. Place in oven and bake 20-25 minutes.

Caramel/Praline Sauce

THIS SAUCE CAN BE USED OVER ICE CREAM, CARAMEL CAKE OR BROWNIE PIE

INGREDIENTS

1 stick of butter
9 oz. of caramel pieces
1 can of Eagle brand milk
½ tsp. of caramel flavoring

DIRECTIONS

1. In a large saucepan over medium heat, melt together the butter, caramel and milk, stirring constantly.
2. When completely melted, add the caramel flavoring and stir well.
3. Cool completely and store in the refrigerator until needed.

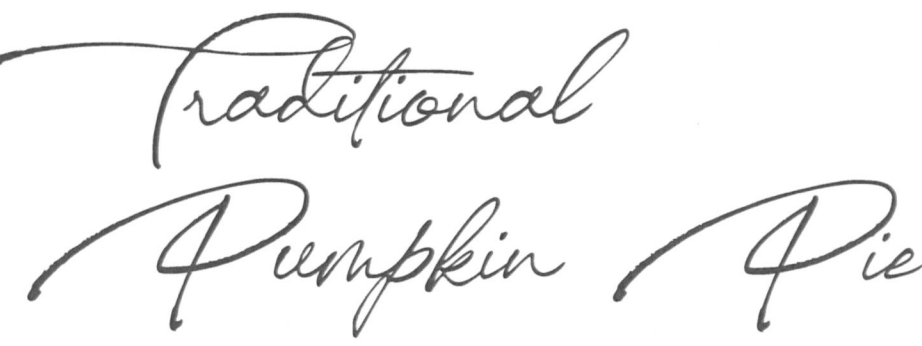

Traditional Pumpkin Pie

Very few people do not request at least a small slice of pumpkin pie after their thanksgiving meal! In our family, it simply isn't Thanksgiving without turkey, stuffing, Sweet Magnolia Rolls, sweet potato casserole, green beans, mashed potatoes, and Pumpkin Pie topped with lots of fresh, real, whipped cream! My great grandchildren just enjoy a serving spoonful of the whipped cream piled in their mouth!

INGREDIENTS

1 unbaked 9" deep dish pie crust (see recipe page 12)
1 can (16 oz.) Libbys pumpkin
1 can (12 oz.) Carnation evaporated milk, (or lactose-free or almond cooking milk)
2 large eggs
¾ cup granulated sugar
1 tsp. ground cinnamon
½ tsp. salt
½ tsp. ground ginger
¼ tsp. ground cloves

DIRECTIONS

1. Preheat oven to 425°.
2. In a small bowl, mix sugar, cinnamon, salt, ginger and cloves.
3. Beat eggs in a large bowl
4. Stir in pumpkin, and sugar-spice mixture.
5. Pour into a Sweet magnolia fresh pie crust.
   Double the recipe to make two holiday pies.
6. Cover the top of the pie crust only with aluminum foil to prevent crust from getting too brown. Bake on middle rack in oven for 15 minutes. Reduce oven temperature to 350° and bake for 40 minutes or until knife inserted in center comes out clean. Cool on wire rack; then refrigerate. Serve with fresh whipped cream!

Cakes

Our families love for cake began with the beautiful and delicious cakes that we baked in the pie shop. Every member of my family developed a different favorite flavor.

Nana perfected the caramel cake and anytime she came to visit, she brought a caramel cake. She would slice it in bite size servings, and we would eat it like candy! She would also serve some little balls of icing that those of us who love icing could binge on! Grandaddy would make sure to offer all of us extra helpings of dinner so he could eat all the cake! Nana would slice him a huge slice of cake (about 1/8th of the cake) and he would eat every bite! He never shared his piece of cake or pie with anyone! He also never gained a pound!

The shop made beautiful triple layer cakes, and sheet cakes of every flavor. If a customer wanted us to make a dessert that we did not offer, I would of course ask them for the recipe and we would make it for them.

The most humorous memory I can recall was a very loyal customer who bought our cakes and pies, but pretended that she had made them. She would even go to the trouble of pulling her car around the back of the pie shop, and we would hand her a Sweet Magnolia bag of desserts out the back door so no one would see her come in the shop! Her husband thought she was a baking phenomenon!

All of my family also bought and carried out many bags of desserts when thy visited. This was one of the many perks of having a bakery in the family. In our family, you cannot have a special occasion or family reunion without cake, pie and homemade rolls! Our holiday memories certainly included our favorite Sweet Magnolia desserts!

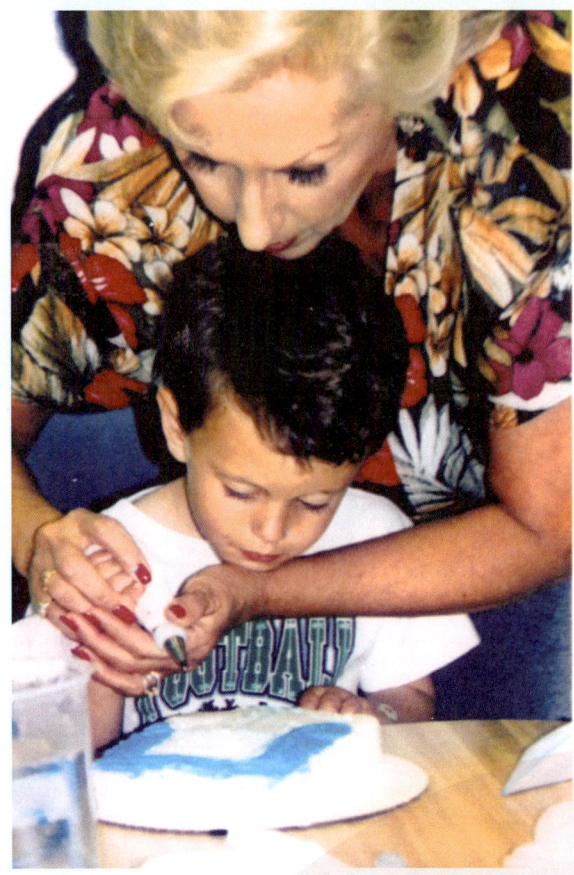

Mimi's Favorite White Cake

INGREDIENTS

2 sheets of wax paper

1 cup and 2 Tbsps. water

4 eggs - separated

1 Duncan Hines Classic White Cake Mix

⅓ cup vegetable oil

1 ½ Tbsps. of vanilla

¼ cup of sour cream

1 tsp. of almond extract

When I was growing up , this was one of the only cakes my mother made. I believe that white cake is best with cream cheese icing. However, it is also wonderful with a delicious homemade buttercream icing. Store bought icing does not have the same fresh sweet taste as a homemade icing!

DIRECTIONS

1. Preheat oven to 350°.
2. Grease two 10" round pans with Bakers Joy non-stick spray.
3. Cut out two 10" round pieces of wax paper and place in bottom of pans.
4. In a large mixing bowl, combine cake mix and water until mixed on low speed.
5. Add the oil and sour cream and mix until smooth.
6. Beat the 4 egg whites and fold into the cake mix.
7. Add vanilla and almond extract.
8. Pour evenly into two cake pans and bake for 25 minutes or until cake springs to the touch. Stick a long toothpick in the center of the cake. It is done when it comes out clean.
9. Cool 10 minutes before turning over and removing the cakes from the pans. You may want to run a knife around the outside edges of the pans to release the cakes.
10. Peel wax paper gently off the cakes
11. For cupcakes, bake 15 minutes - then rotate and cook an additional 3-4 minutes.
12. Ice with Butter Cream or Chocolate Icing (see recipes on pages 80 and 86).

Buttermilk Pound Cake

This buttermilk Pound cake (or "pound bread" as my grandchildren used to call it) has a lighter texture than traditional pound cake. Any pound cake is best eaten by the slice with coffee. However, pound cake can be enjoyed at any time of the day!

INGREDIENTS

2 sticks of butter - diced and chilled

3 cups of sugar

1 ½ tsps. of vanilla

6 eggs

3 cups of flour

½ tsp. of salt

¼ tsp. of baking soda

1 cup buttermilk

DIRECTIONS

1. Preheat oven to 325°.
2. Grease and flour a 10" tube pan. (Or use Bakers instant spray with flour in it) Set aside.
3. Cream together the butter and sugar in a mixer on high speed until fluffy.
4. Add 1 ½ tsp. of vanilla
5. Now using paddle, Add eggs one at a time, blending well. Do not over beat.
6. Sift together the flour, baking soda and salt in a small separate bowl.
7. Add a small portion of the flour mixture to the creamed mixture in the mixer on low speed. Then add a small portion of the buttermilk to the mixer. Keep adding alternatively, ending with the flour mixture.
8. Pour batter into the greased and floured tube pan. Make a trench with a tsp. to ensure the air is not trapped in the batter,
9. Bake approximately 1 hour and 5 minutes. However, make sure you check the cake at around 55 minutes. Different ovens cook at different rates. IF the cake is browning too quickly, place a piece of aluminum foil over the top.
10. To test to see if the cake is done, insert a long toothpick. If it does not come out clean , bake another 2 minutes or until done.
11. Allow the cake to cool for 10 minutes before removing the tube from the pan.
12. Put a plate over the top and flip the cake out. Then quickly turn back over on your cake stand or platter so the top will look pretty! You may dust with some powdered sugar to look pretty.

Old Fashioned Pound Cake

This is my favorite of the two pound cake recipes! At Sweet Magnolia's we served this cake with sliced fresh strawberries and whipped cream as our version of strawberry shortcake. A delicious slice of pound cake is simply delicious and can be enjoyed all year long.

INGREDIENTS

2 sticks of cold butter - diced

3 cups of sugar

2 tsp. of vanilla

6 eggs

1 cup of heavy whipping cream

3 cups of flour

DIRECTIONS

*YOU WILL BE PLACING YOUR CAKE IN A COLD OVEN and then turning oven on!

1. Grease and flour a 10" tube pan. (Or use Bakers instant spray with flour in it) Set aside.
2. Cream together the Butter and Sugar in a mixer on high for 1-2 minutes..
3. Add eggs one at a time and blend together.
4. Add a small portion of the flour mixture to the creamed mixture in the mixer. Then add a small portion of the Whipping Cream to the mixer. Keep adding alternatively, ending with the flour mixture.
5. Add the vanilla and mix well.
6. Pour Batter into a COLD OVEN on Middle Rack and turn oven on 325°. Bake approximately 1 hour and 15 minutes. CHECK YOUR CAKE after one hour. IF the cake is getting brown too quickly, place a piece of aluminum foil loosely over the top.
7. To test to see if the cake is done, tap gently with your fingers in the center of the cake. If it springs back up, it is done. If it not done, bake another 2-3 minutes at a time until done.
8. Allow the cake to cool on a rack or top of a cool area for 10 minutes before removing the cake from the pan.
9. Put a plate over the top and flip the cake out. Then Quickly turn back over on your cake stand or platter so the top will look pretty! You may dust with some powdered sugar to look pretty.

Five Flavor Pound Cake

This luscious moist cake will not disappoint your family or your guests. When you bite into this cake, you can't quite determine what flavor you taste because it has so many active flavors. This pound cake teases your taste buds.

INGREDIENTS

3 sticks butter

3 cups sugar

5 eggs

3 cups flour

½ tsp. baking powder

1 cup milk

5 eggs

1 tsp. coconut extract

1 tsp. rum extract

1 tsp. butter extract

1 tsp. lemon Extract

¼ cup rum

DIRECTIONS

1. Preheat oven to 325°.
2. Spray a 10" tube pan with Bakers Joy Spray and set aside.
3. Cream together the butter and sugar in a mixer on low speed.
4. Add 5 eggs, one at a time, blending just until the yolk breaks.
5. Combine 3 cups of flour and ½ tsp. of baking powder in a small bowl.
6. Alternately add flour mixture and 1 cup milk to creamed mixture.
7. Stir in one tsp. of each: coconut, rum, butter, lemon, and vanilla extracts.
8. Blend in all extracts well.
9. Pour batter into tube pan. Level the batter around with a knife. Make a small trench in the center of the batter to create a more beautiful cake.
10. Place in the preheated oven and bake for 1 hour.
11. Begin making the glaze for the finished cake.

Glaze ingredients and process:
Combine and bring to a boil: ½ cup sugar, ½ tsp. of coconut extract, ½ tsp. of butter extract, ½ tsp. of vanilla extract, ½ tsp. of rum extract, ½ tsp. of lemon extract, ¼ cup of water and ¼ cup of rum. Stir and turn off the burner.

12. After one hour, check cake for doneness by tapping middle of cake gently with your finger. If cake does not spring up when tapped, bake for five to ten more minutes.
13. When cake is done, remove from oven and cool. Turn cake out onto a plate and poke holes in the top of the cake with a toothpick. Slowly Spoon warm glaze over the cake.

Peach Brandy Pound Cake

This heavenly summer cake makes the perfect gift. We sold every pound cake that we made within two days because pound cake is such a versatile and delightful dessert!

INGREDIENTS

2 sticks butter - cold and diced

3 cups sugar

6 eggs

3 cups flour

¼ tsp. baking soda

⅛ tsp. salt

1 cup sour cream

½ cup peach brandy

2 tsps. dark rum

1 tsp. orange extract

1 tsp. vanilla

½ tsp. lemon extract

½ tsp. almond Extract

DIRECTIONS

1. Preheat oven to 325°.
2. Grease a 10" tube pan with Bakers Joy cooking spray.
3. Combine flour, baking soda, and salt in a medium bowl. Set aside.
4. Cream together the butter and sugar on high with whisk.
5. Using paddle, blend in the eggs, one at a time.
6. Add the dry mixture and sour cream alternatively; ending with the flour mixture.
7. Add peach brandy, rum, orange extract, vanilla, lemon extract and almond extract. Stir until blended.
8. Pour batter into the tube pan. Using a Tbsp., make a trench through the middle of the batter.
9. Bake for 1 hour and 20 minutes. Test to see if the cake is done by inserting a toothpick. If the toothpick does not come out clean, bake the cake for another 2 minutes.
10. Allow the cake to cool 10 minutes before removing from the pan.

Chocolate Swirl Pound Cake

This recipe is a chocolate lovers pound cake. The cocoa is just an added bonus to an already delicious dessert. We also served this pound cake drizzled with chocolate sauce to make a pretty presentation.

INGREDIENTS

1 stick of butter - diced and cold

½ cup of vegetable or canola oil

3 cups of sugar

5 large eggs

3 cups of all-purpose flour

½ tsp. of baking powder

¼ tsp. of salt

1 cup of milk

1 tsp. of vanilla

2 Tbsps. of cocoa

DIRECTIONS

1. Preheat oven to 350°.
2. Grease and flour (or use non-stick Baker's spray with flour) a 10" tube pan.
3. Beat the butter and sugar in a mixer until fluffy with whisk on high speed.
4. Add eggs, one at a time. Then add the oil and mix well with a paddle.
5. In another bowl, combine flour, baking powder and salt.
6. Add flour mixture and milk to butter alternatively, beginning and ending with flour mixture
7. Stir in vanilla
8. Remove 2 cups of batter and place in a bowl. Add 2 Tbsps. of Cocoa and stir until blended.
9. Pour ⅓ of plain batter into greased and floured tube pan. Top with half of chocolate mixture. Repeat layers, ending with plain batter. Gently swirl with a knife to create a marble effect.
10. Bake one hour and ten minutes. Test to see if the cake is done by inserting a large toothpick. If it does not come out clean, bake the cake another 2 minutes. Cool 10 minutes before removing from the pan.
11. Put a plate over the tube pan and turn over. Then, gently turn the cake back over onto your cake plate.

Hummingbird Cake

This dense, moist cake is so wonderfully delicious. It contains fresh nuts, bananas and pineapple. Therefore, you can pretend that it is a healthy dessert! It doesn't even have to be iced to be delicious!

INGREDIENTS

3 cups Hudsons all-purpose flour

2 cups sugar

1 tsp. baking soda

1 tsp. salt

1 tsp. cinnamon

3 eggs

1 cup chopped pecan pieces

1 cup vegetable oil

1 ½ tsps. Watkins vanilla

1 tsp. butter flavoring

1 cup undrained crushed pineapple

2 cups gently mashed bananas

Powdered sugar - optional on top

DIRECTIONS

1. Preheat oven to 350°.
2. Cut two pieces of wax paper in circles to fit the bottom only of the round cake pans. Then spray with Bakers Joy non-stick spray. (This keeps cakes from sticking to the pan. Gently Peel wax paper off of cakes after you turn out cakes on plates). You may also use a greased Bundt pan.
3. In a large mixer, place the flour, sugar, baking soda, salt and cinnamon and stir with a paddle.
4. Beat Eggs in another small bowl with a whisk.
5. Add eggs and oil to flour mixture and stir just until moist.
6. Add the vanilla, butter flavoring, undrained crushed pineapple, chopped pecans, and mashed bananas and stir together.
7. Pour mixture into the two round cake pans or one bundt pan (your choice).
8. Bake for 35-45 minutes and then check cake by pressing on the top of the cake with your finger. If it bounces back up, cakes are done. If it is not quite done, continue baking another 5 minutes. Repeat checking until cake is done.
9. Allow cake to cool for 10 minutes before flipping onto plate or counter.
10. When cakes are completely cool, frost with cream cheese Icing (see recipe page 81) or dust with powdered sugar.

Big Don's Favorite Red Velvet Cake

This three layer beautiful cake is served every year at our families' Christmas celebration! It is a dense, very moist beautiful red cake, and we ice it with fresh homemade cream cheese icing. It is so heavenly, you can't eat just one piece!

INGREDIENTS

2 sticks butter

1 ½ cups water

¾ cup of vegetable oil

¾ cup of buttermilk

1 ½ tsps. baking soda

3 cups sugar

¾ cup cocoa

3 cups Hudson's all-purpose flour

3 eggs

1 ½ tsps. of vanilla

⅛ cup of red food coloring

Wax paper

2 round cake pans for double layer cake

DIRECTIONS

1. Preheat oven to 350°.
2. Cut wax paper into two 10" circles and place in the bottom of two 10" round pans. Grease the lined pans with Baker's Joy non-stick spray.
3. Place Sugar, flour and cocoa in a mixing bowl and stir together. Set aside.
4. Combine slightly beaten eggs with the vanilla and food coloring and set aside.
5. Pour Buttermilk into a ¾ cup measuring cup. Measure out 1 ½ tsps. of baking soda. Set both aside.
6. In a medium saucepan, bring the butter, water and vegetable oil to a boil. Add to the flour/sugar/cocoa mixture. Then add the egg/vanilla/food coloring mixture.
7. Combine the Buttermilk and Baking soda and stir. Mix into the rest of batter and pour into cake pans evenly.
8. Place cake pans on middle rack in oven and bake for 20 minutes..
9. Gently pat down any bubbles with an oven Mitt while cooking.
10. Check after 20 minutes by patting down gently in the center of cakes , if they bounce back up, they are done. If not ready, bake for 5-more minute intervals and check for doneness, Remove from oven when top of cakes bounce bake when touched with finger gently. Cover with a clean kitchen towel. Allow cakes to cool for 10 minutes before removing from pan. Chill cakes in refrigerator before icing. Cakes ice better if cold. Cakes may also be wrapped well and frozen until ready to ice at another time. Let cakes sit out of freezer for an hour before icing.
11. Ice cakes with cream cheese Icing (see recipe page 81) that has been chilled for 10 minutes.

Carrot Cake (1/2 SHEET)

Carrot Cake is a very popular, healthy cake. Freshly grated carrots, raisins, coconut, pecans and crushed pineapple make this a wholesome, yummy dessert!

INGREDIENTS

2 ½ cups sugar
2 ½ cups all-purpose flour
2 ½ tsps. baking soda
¾ tsp. salt
¾ tsps. cinnamon
1 cup diced carrots
5 eggs
¼ cup raisins (optional)
¼ cup coconut
¼ cup chopped pecans (optional)
1 (4 oz.) can of crushed pineapple
1 cup oil
1 cup buttermilk
2 ¼ tsps. vanilla extract
¼ tsp. orange extract

DIRECTIONS

1. Preheat oven to 350°. For ½ sheet cake. 350° for 10" rounds.
2. Grease two 10" round pans or one 9"x13" pan with Bakers Joy Non Stick Spray. (If using round pans, cut 2 round pieces of wax paper to fit bottom of round pans so cakes will not stick to round pans).
3. In a mixing bowl, mix together the dry ingredients and set aside.
4. With a hand mixer, whip eggs lightly.
5. Mix in oil, buttermilk, vanilla and orange extract on low or by hand.
6. Add Dry ingredients to mixing bowl.
7. Stir in pineapple pecans, and coconut individually and blend well.
8. Pour batter into 9"x13" pan or two 10" rounds and bake approximately 30 minutes.
   Insert small toothpick in center of cake to check if it is done. If toothpick comes out clean, cake is done. Allow cake to cool for 10 minutes before removing from pan.
9. Ice cake with cream cheese icing (see recipe on page 81).

Fresh Strawberry Cake

Young and old love a fresh strawberry cake. We made many wedding cakes using this moist delightful recipe. However, it can also be enjoyed as an everyday family dessert.

INGREDIENTS

1 box of Duncan Hines white cake mix

4 egg whites

1 Tbsp. of white vanilla

1 cup water

⅓ cup vegetable oil

¼ cup of sour cream

1 Tbsp. of strawberry extract

1 cup diced fresh strawberries

DIRECTIONS

1. Preheat oven to 350°.
2. Spray pans lightly with Joy Baking Spray. Cut parchment paper circles and place in the bottom of your two 10" pans or spray a 9"x13" pan.
3. In mixing bowl, combine all ingredients and blend well on medium.
4. Bake cakes 25 minutes at 350°, then check. Cake will be done when it springs up after you press lightly on the middle of cake with your finger. If it needs more time, rotate cakes and bake an additional 2 minutes and check.
5. *If baking in a 9"x13" inch pan, it may require 25-35 minutes to cook.
6. You can ice with butter cream icing (see recipe page 80) or strawberry icing (see recipe below).

Fresh Strawberry Cake Icing

INGREDIENTS

1 stick butter, softened

1 tsp. lemon juice

1 Tbsp. strawberry flavoring

¾ cup fresh diced strawberries

3-4 cups of powered sugar (or more)

DIRECTIONS

1. Cream butter in a mixer. Gradually add powdered sugar until blended. Add lemon juice and strawberry flavoring. Add more powdered sugar to thicken icing if needed. Add diced fresh strawberries and stir by hand. Spread over your refrigerated 9"x13" cake or two round stacked cakes.

Italian Cream Cake

If you love coconut, you will love this cake! It is a moist delectable dessert loaded with coconut flavor and toasted pecans!.

INGREDIENTS

2 - 10" round cake pans

2 sheets of wax paper

2 ¼ cups of sugar

1 stick of butter

¾ cup of vegetable oil

¾ cup of sour cream, 6 oz.

2 ½ cups of all-purpose flour

2 tsps. of baking soda

1 cup of whole buttermilk

2 Tbsps. of vanilla

½ cups of coconut

¼ cups of toasted coconut

5 eggs - room temperature. Separate the yolks from the whites (save the whites)

1 ½ cups of chopped toasted pecans (Toast pecans in the oven on a cookie sheet at 350° for about 10 minutes or until golden brown)

DIRECTIONS

1. Preheat oven to 325°.
2. Spray pans with Bakers Joy Non-Stick spray with flour. Cut wax paper in round circles to fit the bottom of your 2 cake pans.
3. Separate egg yolks from whites.
4. Combine and cream the sugar and butter in mixer.
5. Add the oil and sour cream and mix on regular speed for 5 minutes.
6. Mix in the 5 egg yolks, just until blended.
7. In a separate bowl blend together the 2 ½ cups of flour and 2 tsps. of baking soda.
8. Alternatively, add the buttermilk and flour mixture - ending with flour mixture.
9. Fold in the vanilla, coconut, toasted coconut and pecans.
10. Beat room temperature egg whites until creamy (1-2 minutes) and fold beaten egg whites into the batter.
11. Pour the batter into 2 cake pans - divided evenly.
12. Bake for 25-30 minutes. Then check cakes to see if they are done by pressing lightly on the top of the cake. If it springs back up it is done. Cakes do not have to look golden brown when they are done. If they need more time, rotate pans in the oven and bake 5 -10 minutes more and check again!
13. Allow cakes to cool for 10 minutes before removing from pans.
14. May ice with either buttercream icing or cream. (see pages 80 and 81)

Buttercream Icing

INGREDIENTS

½ cup solid vegetable shortening

½ cup (1 stick) butter, softened

4 cups sifted powdered sugar (confectioners sugar)

2 Tbsps. milk , heavy cream or water

1 tsp. vanilla extract (pure is best)

DIRECTIONS

1. In an electric mixing bowl, fitted with paddle attachment, cream the butter and shortening on medium speed until light and fluffy. Beat in the vanilla and scrape down the bowl occasionally.

2. Gradually add powdered sugar, one cup at a time. When all the sugar has been mixed in the icing will seem dry and stiff.

3. Add vanilla and stir.

4. Gradually add small amounts of milk or cream until the desired icing consistency is reached. Continue to beat until icing is light and fluffy.

*To Make Strawberry Icing

Add: 1 Tbsp. strawberry flavoring and ¾ cup of diced strawberries

Cream Cheese Icing

INGREDIENTS

2 sticks of butter

4 cups (plus) of powdered sugar

2 Tbsps. of vanilla

2 (8 oz.) blocks of cream cheese (softened)

DIRECTIONS

1. Place butter and cream cheese in a mixing bowl - using the blending paddle, not whisk. Blend on low speed.
2. Add vanilla and 4 cups of powdered sugar, one cup at a time. If necessary, add a little more powdered sugar until thick so it spreads easily. If you want it to be a little stiffer, place in refrigerator 15 minutes before icing your cake.

German Chocolate Cake

This divine dessert is often overlooked nowadays because not everyone loves pineapple or coconut. However, if you are a fan of these flavors, surprise your family or guests with this rare scrumptious cake.

INGREDIENTS

½ cup water

4 oz. German chocolate

2 cups sugar

1 cup butter

4 eggs

1 tsp. vanilla

2 ½ cups cake flour

1 tsp. baking soda

¼ tsp. salt

1 cup buttermilk

DIRECTIONS

1. Preheat oven to 350°.
2. Grease two 10" round cake pans with Bakers Joy non-stick spray.
3. Sift together the cake flour, baking soda, salt and set aside.
4. Boil water in saucepan and bring to boil. Add German chocolate bars and stir until melted. Remove from heat.
5. In a mixer, cream together the sugar and butter.
6. Separate egg yolks from whites and reserve whites for later.
7. Add egg yolks, one at a time to sugar mixture.
8. Blend the vanilla and chocolate mixture into creamed mixture.
9. Add flour mixture and buttermilk alternatively, starting and ending with flour mixture.
10. Beat egg whites with a hand beater until stiff, not dry. Gently fold the egg whites into the batter with a spatula.
11. Pour batter into 2 cake pans and spread evenly.
12. Bake cakes on middle rack in oven for 20 minutes or until done. You can test cakes by gently pressing the top of the cakes with your fingers. If cakes bounce back, the cakes are done. If cakes are not done, bake an additional 2 minutes and check cakes again. Continue checking until cakes are done.
13. Cool cakes 10 minutes before turning over on your board or counter.
14. Take a knife gently run around the pan to loosen cake from pan. Flip cake out on your board or counter.
15. Make icing while cakes are cooling. When cakes are cool, ice cake between layers and on top of top layer for a traditional German Chocolate Cake. (Make more icing if icing the whole cake).

German Chocolate Icing

INGREDIENTS

1 ½ cups butter

3 cups dark brown sugar

1 cup evaporated milk

1 tsp. vanilla

3 cups fresh flaked coconut

2 ¼ cups chopped pecan

1 cup crushed pineapple, drained

DIRECTIONS

In a saucepan, melt together the butter, milk, brown sugar, vanilla, and pineapple. Stir in the coconut and chopped nuts. Ice the top layers of cakes.

Chocolate Fudge Cake

I first ate this cake when visiting my Aunt Dede who was a fabulous cook! She made this chocolate "heaven" every time we visited her. I copied her good sense and prepare this cake more than any other in my day-to-day life because it is an easy and very delicious way to spoil my family and friends!

INGREDIENTS

1 stick of butter

1 cup of Coke or water

½ cup of vegetable oil

2 cups of sugar

2 cups of flour

4-5 Tbsps. cocoa

2 eggs

1 or 2 tsps. of vanilla

½ cup of buttermilk

1 tsp. of baking soda

*If making a two layer cake, double recipe

DIRECTIONS

1. Preheat oven to 375° oven.
2. Spray one 9"x13" cake pan or two 10" round pans with Bakers Joy Non-stick Spray.
3. Combine the Sugar, Flour, and Cocoa in a mixing bowl and set aside.
4. Combine the eggs and vanilla in another small separate bowl.
5. Place butter, coke and vegetable oil in a 2 quart saucepan. Stir and melt together. Set off the burner.
6. Add the hot ingredients to your mixing bowl and stir thoroughly together.
7. Add egg mixture to the mixing bowl.
8. Stir the baking soda into the buttermilk and then add to the mixing bowl. Mix well.
9. Pour batter into the greased and floured pan.
10. Bake for approximately 20-25 minutes. Test the cake to see if it is done by inserting a toothpick. If it comes out clean, it is done. If not, bake 2 more minutes and check again.
11. Allow the cake to cool for 10 minutes before removing from the pan.
12. Ice with fudge frosting (see recipe page 86).

Chocolate Fudge Icing For Chocolate Fudge Cake

INGREDIENTS

For 9"x13" cake
Spread on warm cake
and then let set up

1 stick of butter
4-5 Tbsps. cocoa
6 Tbsps. Coke (or milk if preferred)
1 box (32 oz.) of powdered sugar
1-2 tsp. vanilla
1 cup of chopped pecans (optional)
*For a double layer cake, double recipe

DIRECTIONS

1. Stir in a sauce pan the first three ingredients until the butter is melted. Do not boil.
2. Remove from heat and add the vanilla.
3. Gradually, add the powdered sugar using a hand mixer, and quickly blend until the consistency is thick and spreadable, but not grainy and stiff.
4. If frosting gets too thick, you can add a Tbsp. of milk and stir.
5. Add nuts last and spread over warm 9"x13" cake.

*If icing 2 layer cake, chill cakes before icing so icing does not melt and run off cake.

Jam Cake

This is not your everyday fruitcake! This seasonal dessert is made with fresh ingredients and blackberry jam, not typical dried fruit! During the holidays, we made this cake in loaves and bundt pans and iced each with rich caramel icing. We sold so many of these small jam cakes to customers to give as gifts.

INGREDIENTS

1 cup vegetable oil

2 cups sugar

3 eggs

1 cup buttermilk

2 cups of self-rising flour

½ tsp. nutmeg

1 Tbsp. cinnamon

3 Tbsps. of cocoa

1 ½ cups of chopped walnuts

1 ½ cups of blackberry jam

3 Tbsps. of Carnation condensed milk

DIRECTIONS

1. Preheat oven to 350°.
2. Spray Tube pan or 2 small round pans with Bakers Joy non-stick Spray. Set aside.
3. In a small mixing bowl, stir together the self-rising flour, nutmeg, cinnamon, and walnuts.
4. In a mixer, cream together the oil and sugar.
5. Add eggs one at a time and beat well.
6. Add 1 cup of buttermilk.
7. Add the jam and mix well.
8. Stir in the condensed milk.
9. Pour batter into the Tube pan and bake for 45 minutes on a narrow tray.
10. Rotate Tube pan and bake another 40- 45 minutes. Check about five minutes before done by inserting a long toothpick. If it comes out clean, remove the cake from the oven. If not, bake for 2 more minutes or until toothpick comes out clean.
11. Allow cake to cool for 10 minutes before removing from pan. When completely cool, frost with caramel icing (see recipe page 90).

White Chocolate Cake

This is a very sweet and piquant cake. It does require a bit more preparation time so enjoy making this on a relaxed fall or winter day. It is perfect for a ladies' coffee or afternoon tea, and it may just become a favorite!

INGREDIENTS

2 ½ cups cake flour
½ tsp. salt
1 tsp. baking soda
1 cup butter
2 cups sugar
4 egg yolks
½ cup of water
4 oz. white chocolate
2 Tbsps. vegetable oil
½ tsp. vanilla
1 cup buttermilk

DIRECTIONS

1. Preheat oven to 350°.
2. Lightly grease two round 10" pans with Baker's Joy non-stick spray.
3. Sift the flour, salt, and baking soda in a small bowl.
4. In electric mixer, cream the butter and sugar until fluffy.
5. Separate egg yolks from whites. Add 4 egg yolks only – one at a time into the mixing bowl and blend well. Set aside the whites for later.
6. Boil ½ cup of water in a saucepan. Add the White chocolate to the hot water and stir until thoroughly melted.
7. Add the oil and vanilla to saucepan and stir.
8. Alternatively, blend in the flour mixture and the buttermilk into the mixing bowl containing the creamed mixture.
9. Whip egg whites with a hand mixer until stiff and then gently fold into creamed mixture with a spoon.
10. Evenly distribute batter into the two 10" round cake pans and spread evenly or pour batter into a 9"X13" greased pan.
11. Put pans in the oven and bake for 22 minutes. (30-40 minutes if using a 9"x13"pan). Check to see if cake is done by gently pressing down on the top of the cake with your fingers. If it bounces back, it is done. If it is not done, bake another 2 minutes and check again. Cool for 10 minutes before turning cake out on a board or counter.
12. Ice bottom cake completely, and then place top layer on and ice top layer. Ice cake with your favorite icing!

Easy Apple Pecan Cake

This was a delicious holiday cake. We made these cakes in bundt pans and decorated them with gum drops and brightly colored candy to look like beautiful Christmas wreaths.

INGREDIENTS

1 cup oil

3 eggs - slightly beaten

2 cups sifted self-rising flour

2 cups sugar

1 Tbsp. cinnamon

1 Tbsp. nutmeg

3 cups of chopped apples

1 Tbsp. vanilla

1 cup of pecan pieces

DIRECTIONS

1. Spray a bundt pan with Bakers Joy baking spray.
2. Preheat oven to 350°.
3. Add all ingredients together and blend.
4. Pour batter into the greased bundt pan and bake for 50 minutes.
5. Check after 45 minutes by taping cake gently with your finger. If cake springs up, cake is done. If not, cook about another 5 minutes or until done.
6. Allow the cake to cool for 10 minutes and then turn out of pan on a plate.
7. Ice the cake with cream cheese icing (see recipe page 81) or dust with powdered sugar.

Easy Penuche Frosting

(CARAMEL)

This icing is best by the spoonful! My mother would prepare an iced caramel cake every time she visited us. She would also bring a tray of icing "balls" for us to enjoy along side our cake.

INGREDIENTS

½ cup butter or margarine
1 cup packed brown sugar
¼ cup milk
2 cups powdered sugar
*Can double ingredients to make extra frosting!

DIRECTIONS

1. Heat butter in a medium saucepan until melted.
2. Stir in brown sugar.
3. Heat to boiling, stirring constantly. Boil and stir over low heat for 2 minutes.
4. Stir in milk; heat to boiling.
5. Remove pan from heat and cool until lukewarm.
6. Stir in powdered sugar gradually.
7. Beat with mixer until frosting is smooth and spreading consistency. If frosting becomes too stiff to spread on cake, you can add a very small amount of HOT water and stir.

NOTE: This recipe frosts two 8" or 9" layers or the top of a 13"x9" inch cake.

Kentucky Bourbon Cake

INGREDIENTS

1 yellow cake mix
½ cup instant vanilla pudding mix
4 eggs
½ cup of oil
1 cup of milk
2 Tbsps. of bourbon
1 cup of chopped pecans

Glaze
1 stick of butter
1 cup of sugar
½ cup bourbon

DIRECTIONS

1. Preheat oven to 325°.
2. Grease and flour a bundt pan.
3. In a mixing bowl, combine all ingredients together and blend with a mixer on medium speed for one minute.
4. Pour batter into bundt pan and bake for 45 minutes. You may need to cover the bundt pan with foil the last 10 minutes if the cake browns too fast before it is completely done.
5. While the cake is cooling, bring to a boil the butter, sugar and bourbon in a saucepan. Boil glaze sauce for 2 minutes. Remove from heat.
6. When cake is cool, turn cake out onto a serving plate. With a toothpick, poke holes all over the top of cake and sides. Pour the glaze slowly over the cake to allow the glaze to seep down into the cake.

Rum Cake

This recipe was Grandaddy Walden's favorite! He could eat the whole cake in one day. This yummy moist cake is perfect enjoyed with your morning coffee or a late night snack!

INGREDIENTS

Recipe makes 1 Cake

1 yellow cake mix

4 eggs

½ cup instant vanilla pudding mix, 3 ⅝ oz.

½ cup of water

¼ cup of vegetable or canola oil

½ cup of finely chopped pecans

½ cup of dark rum

Rum Glaze

1 stick of butter

½ cup of water

1 cup of sugar

½ cup of rum

DIRECTIONS

1. Preheat oven to 325° and bake on middle rack.
2. Grease and flour (or spray with Bakers Joy Non-Stick Spray) one 10" bundt pan.
3. Sprinkle ½ cup pecans into the bottom of the greased bundt pan.
4. In a mixing bowl, combine all other cake ingredients and blend with electric mixer for 3 minutes.
5. Pour batter into bundt pan and bake for 45 minutes. Test cake at 35 minutes. Cake will be done when cake bounces back up when pressed gently with index finger on top.
6. When cake is done and cooling on a rack, bring to boil the butter, water and sugar for Glaze on medium heat. Allow Glaze to boil for 2 minutes.
7. Take off heat and add ½ cup of rum and stir in on low.
8. When cake has cooled on wire rack for 10 minutes, run a knife gently around the outside of bundt pan to loosen the cake from pan. Turn bundt pan over on your serving plate and pat gently on bottom of pan to loosen the cake and allow it to fall onto your plate.
9. Take a toothpick and punch lots of holes in the bottom of your cake so the rum glaze will soak into the cake. Slowly pour glaze over your warm cake.

The Wedding Cake

Many customers had asked us to make their wedding cake. However, I did not like the taste of fondant icing so I was very reluctant. Then I met Jode Rose at a Lexington Christian Academy ballgame. She was a friend of my daughter Michelle and her husband Ross. Jode's daughter was also a good friend of my granddaughter Sarah Beth. Jode happened to be an expert in fondant iced cakes and so she agreed to come and work with me. Jode made beautiful fondant cakes of all kinds. For one customer's birthday, she made a cake in the shape of a Louis Vuitton purse! Jode worked with me for many years and made many beautiful cakes for birthdays or special occasions upon request! She made one wedding cake for a very elaborate wedding that we sold for $2,500.

Jode baked this 1957 Chevy Cake to celebrate Don Moore Automotive's 100 years in business. My son in law 's family car business, Don Moore Automotive, has been in business for 102 years in Owensboro Kentucky.

LIFE IS SHORT, EAT DESSERT FIRST   JACQUES TORRES

Cupcakes

Most children prefer cupcakes to a cake or pie. In fact, I don't know many people who don't love a fresh cupcake. Our bakery made cupcakes in every cake variety we baked. We made sure that we carried several varieties in our cooler on any day.

White Cupcakes with buttercream icing were my grandchildren's favorite dessert when they were children. My son Micheal and his wife Emily would bring their two children, Macey and Trey, to the pie shop every Saturday afternoon when they lived in Lexington. We would ice and decorate cupcakes all afternoon for them to take home. I would pull out every decoration we stocked, and we would have a wonderful time creating cupcakes and making memories.

My daughter Michelle's three children, who lived in Lexington, grew up visiting, helping, and working at the Pie Shoppe. They stopped by often through the years just to get their favorite dessert. They had birthday parties at the shoppe and even school field trips. The kids and their friends had so much fun! When Ryan, Sarah Beth and Taylor were older they worked out front during the Thanksgiving and Christmas rush. Michelle worked at the shoppe, first with payroll and later with baking. I also sent many desserts to Lexington Christian Academy, for their school functions. I am so thankful for all of the ways in which I was able to help and grace my family with love and "şweetness". These memories are what I value most about owning and managing my dessert business.

Cookies & Bars

Sweet Magnolia really expanded its sales of cookies and bars when my Son-in-law opened up a coffee shop, Overflow café, beside his Chevrolet/Cadillac showroom on Highway 54 in Owensboro, Kentucky. My daughter, Marla, son-in-law, Don, granddaughter, Ashley and her husband, Ronnie wanted to open a coffee shop for the customers to enjoy while getting their cars serviced. Don and Marla thought they needed some sweets to add to the coffee shop menu for employees to enjoy and customers to taste while waiting for their car to be serviced, or delivered. They agreed that my Sweet Magnolia desserts was the obvious, most delicious way to compliment the coffee menu.

To this day, every service customer receives a free coffee token and an invitation to enjoy relaxing in the Overflow coffee shop. The Sweet Magnolia bars, cakes, pies, chicken salad, and pimiento cheese were favorites of their many customers during the last ten years of my pie business. Every week, Fred May or John Stavrakis would drive three hours to Lexington and pick up a few cakes, three or four pies, and sheets of lemon, chess, and pecan bars, plus brownies. Susan and her employees would slice the dessert sheets into 2 inch bars and place them in their beautiful, glass display refrigerator. Overflow coffee shop became quite popular as much for the slices of dessert as for their delicious hand crafted coffee. In addition to complimenting the overflow menu, Marla and Don's favorite perk of having my Sweet Magnolia dessert shop at their disposal, was having desserts for their annual summer company Party in August, and having the opportunity to order desserts from the pie shop for any party or shower they were hosting in Owensboro.

Don and Carol Moore, my son-in-laws parents, hosted the annual Don Moore Automotive company picnic on their farm in Maceo, Kentucky. The 200 employees and their families that attended looked forward to the dessert cart after the meal. Moonlite Barbecue catered the picnic every year, and the Moore Family would make some homemade casseroles to accompany the wonderful food display. After the barbecue dinner was over, the Sweet Magnolia desserts were arranged on an old flat bed truck that was painted hunter green with a red and white fringed canopy top. I delivered the desserts fresh from Lexington to the picnic for many years to make sure they sliced and served the desserts the "correct" way. Believe it or not, there is an art to slicing and serving a pie and cake. The Moore's would carry out at least ten triple layer cakes, ten pies, and beautiful trays piled with dessert bars. Of course, All of this was served with ice cream! To this day my daughter, Marla's favorite Don Moore Automotive memory is of the summer company party followed by the covered wagon full of beautiful and delicious Sweet Magnolia desserts to spoil the Don Moore Employees.

Ribbon cutting for the Overflow Cafe' Coffee Shop at Don Moore Chevrolet in Owensboro. We "spoiled" their customers with Sweet Magnolia Pies, Cakes, and Dessert Bars with a cup of coffee as they serviced their cars. They still serve and sell our delicious chicken salad recipe to lucky customers!

LIFE IS SHORT, EAT DESSERT FIRST   JACQUES TORRES

Sugar Cookie Dough

In my pie kitchen, we made thousands of hand decorated cut-out cookies for birthdays, Easter, Halloween, and Christmas. We sold every cookie we made because our sugar cookies were so exquisite and scrumptious! We hand decorated each cookie with brightly colored candies, icing, and tiny edible decorations.

INGREDIENTS

5 ½ cups all-purpose flour

1 tsp. salt

6 sticks butter

3 cups sugar

1 Tbsp. plus

1 tsp. of vanilla

4 eggs

DIRECTIONS

1. Set out butter a few hours prior to making cookies.
2. Preheat oven to 325°.
3. Combine the flour and salt in a small bowl and set aside.
4. In a mixer, cream the butter and sugar.
5. Add 4 eggs to the butter mixture in mixer.
6. Add the vanilla: Do not over mix!
7. Gather dough together and make several Round balls. Refrigerate for a few hours or overnight or freeze for later use.) Dough should still be chilled before rolling out!
8. Grease your hands lightly so they don't stick to dough.
9. Roll out the cookie dough on a lightly floured board to ¼ inch to ½ inch thickness and then cut with cookie cutter shapes.
10. Bake on an ungreased cookie sheet for 8 minutes. However, check on them before the 8 minutes is up. You will want them to be just slightly brown around the edges.
11. Remove from the cookie sheet with a large metal spatula. Allow the cookies to cool lying flat on a cutting board or clean flat surface.
12. Ice them if desired and decorate.

Million Dollar Cookies

A customer gave me this recipe to try. She received the cookie recipe when she was lunching at Neiman Marcus in New York City. They gave out the recipe when you ordered the cookies for dessert.

INGREDIENTS

2 sticks butter – set out of refrigerator until slightly soft to the touch, but not warm or melted.

1 cup sugar

1 cup brown sugar

2 eggs

1 tsp. Watkins vanilla

1 ¼ cup flour

2 ½ cups oatmeal

1 tsp. salt

1 tsp. baking powder

1 tsp. baking soda

12 oz. semi-sweet chocolate chips

4 oz. grated Hershey Bar (optional)

1 ½ cup chopped walnuts

DIRECTIONS

1. Preheat oven to 330°.
2. Place the flour, oatmeal, salt, baking powder, and soda in a medium bowl and stir together. Set aside.
3. Cream together the butter and sugar in mixer. Do not over beat.
4. Add eggs and vanilla and stir.
5. Add dry ingredients to mixing bowl and stir together.
6. Add chocolate chips, grated Hershey Bar, and nuts. Stir together.
7. Chill dough in refrigerator if dough gets too soft or to make sure cookies bake up thick and pretty.
8. Spoon one Tbsp. in a ball and place 2 inches apart on a cookie sheet.
9. Bake for 8-10 minutes or until just golden brown around edges. Do not over-bake! Cookies will not look golden on top.
10. Allow to cool for 5 minutes. Then, remove from pan with a spatula and allow to cool on counter.

Triple Chocolate Cookies

INGREDIENTS

4 oz. bar chocolate

1 ½ cups chocolate chips

2 sticks butter, room temperature

4 eggs

1 ¼ Tbsps. vanilla

3 cups flour

2 cups semi-sweet chocolate chips

½ cup milk chocolate chips

1 cups of white chocolate, chopped or white chocolate chips

2 cups of chopped walnuts

DIRECTIONS

1. Preheat oven to 325°.
2. Melt the bar chocolate and chocolate chips in a microwave.
3. Place the melted chocolate mixture, butter, eggs and vanilla in a mixing bowl and blend until mixed together.
4. Add the flour to mixing bowl and blend together.
5. Stir in the semi-sweet and milk chocolate chips.
6. Stir in the 2 cups of chopped walnuts.
7. Roll 1 Tbsp. of dough into a ball and press down with a fork into a flat disk.
8. Refrigerate disks an hour or so before baking to retain shape or freeze until needed. If frozen, you can bake right out of the freezer.
9. Bake disks in oven for 7 minutes, turn and bake 2 more minutes.

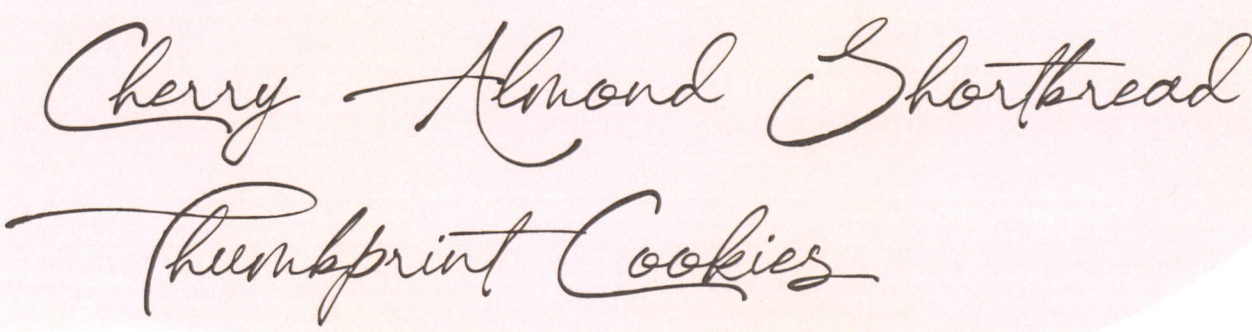

Cherry Almond Shortbread Thumbprint Cookies

This is a wonderful recipe to prepare with grandchildren. These cookies are easy to make, and children will love filling the center with the raspberry jam.

INGREDIENTS

⅔ cup of sugar

1 cup of salted butter, softened

2 cups of all-purpose flour

½ tsp. of almond extract

½ cup of raspberry jam

1 cup of powdered Sugar

1 ½ tsp. almond extract

2-3 tsps. water

DIRECTIONS

1. Heat Oven to 350°.
2. In bowl of large mixer, combine the sugar, butter, and almond extract. Beat at medium speed until creamy (2-3 minutes)
3. Reduce speed to low and add flour gradually. Beat well until mixed (2-3 minutes). Cover and chill dough at least 1 hour.
4. Shape the dough into 1 inch balls. Place 2 inches apart on a cookie sheet.
5. With thumb, make an indention in the center of each cookie (edges may crack slightly). Fill each center with about ¼ tsp. jam.
6. Bake for 12 to 18 minutes or until edges are lightly browned. Let stand one minute, and then remove from the cookie sheet. Cool.
7. Meanwhile, in a small bowl, whisk together the powdered sugar, Almond extract and water until smooth. Brush this over the cookies.
8. Makes 3 ½ dozen cookies.

Date Walnut Double Decker Bars

I have made these bars my whole life. We sold these bars during the Holidays because the taste of dates baked on a cookie crust is an enticing festive treat!

INGREDIENTS

2 ½ cups of sifted all-purpose flour

⅔ cup of sugar

2 sticks of softened butter

⅔ cup of light brown sugar

⅔ cup of sugar

4 eggs

2 tsps. of vanilla extract

4 Tbsps. of flour

2 tsps. of baking powder

1 tsp. of salt

½ tsp. of nutmeg

2 cups of chopped walnuts

2 cups of chopped dates

DIRECTIONS

1. Preheat oven to 350°.
2. Combine and blend the flour, sugar and softened butter into fine crumbs with a pastry blender.
3. Press the mixture into the bottom of a greased 9"x13" cake pan. Bake 20 minutes or until edges are lightly brown.
4. Combine and mix well with a spoon the brown sugar, ⅔ cup of sugar, eggs and vanilla.
5. Sift together the 4 Tbsps. of flour and 2 tsps. of baking powder.
6. Add the salt and nutmeg to the flour mixture.
7. Combine the flour mixture and the sugar mixture with a spoon.
8. Add the walnuts and dates.
9. Pour the batter over the baked crust and bake another 20 minutes. Allow the bars to completely cool in the pan and then remove by turning over the whole pan onto a cutting board.
10. Sprinkle the top of the bars with powdered sugar and cut into 2"x4" bars.

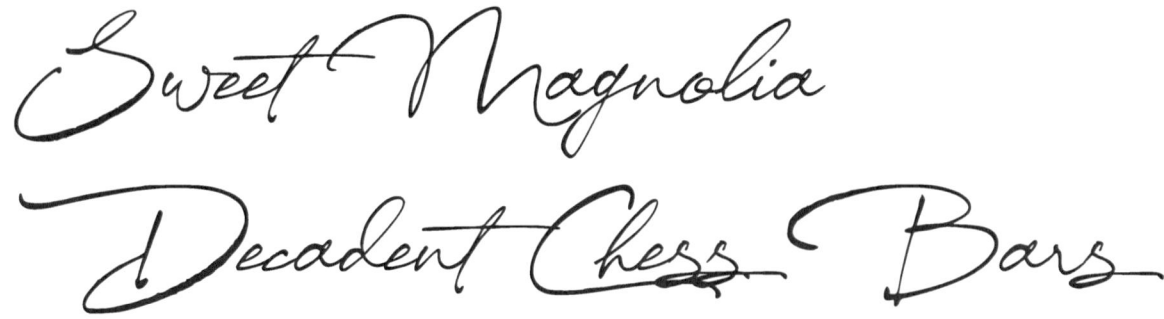

Sweet Magnolia Decadent Chess Bars

These scrumptious gooey dessert bars were a favorite cookie in our pie shop. We included the chess, Pecan, brownie, and fudgy peanut butter bars in a sampler tray that we sold so that our customers could try different kinds of bars.

*Baking Notes: Set cream cheese out 1 hour before you begin cooking.

INGREDIENTS

1 Duncan Hines Yellow Cake Mix
4 medium eggs - whipped
8 oz cream cheese – softened
4 cups powdered sugar- sifted
1 stick (½ cup) cold butter -
cut in small squares

DIRECTIONS

Topping

1. Add softened cream cheese to the clean mixing bowl and blend slowly with the paddle. Add eggs and blend. Add sifted powdered sugar. Blend slowly with paddle. Make sure there are no lumps in the mixture.
2. Pour the topping over the baked crust.
3. Place in a 325° oven and bake for 20 minutes or more until topping is golden brown. Check regularly so you don't over-bake! Cool and cut in squares.

Crust Process

1. Spray a 9"x13" inch pan with Joy Baking Spray. Then line sides and bottom of pan with wax paper
2. With a Pastry Blender, blend the cake mix and diced butter in a bowl.
3. Transfer the flour mixture to an Electric mixer and blend in 2 eggs using the paddle. Scrape the sides of the mixing bowl and push into the egg/flour/butter mixture. (Note: If flour mixture is too thick to form a ball, add a tsp. of beaten egg.)
4. Mold the dough into a log shape and place on a 16" long piece of Parchment Paper. (Use the inch measuring squares on the parchment paper to ensure that your parchment is a 16"piece.). Mark the center of your bottom parchment to indicate 9"X13". Cover the dough with another 16" piece of parchment and proceed to roll the dough into a 9"x13" rectangle. The dough from the center out like a pie crust until the dough is a 9"x13" rectangle. Take off Top piece of parchment only. Lift into the baking pan. Mold the edges into the corners of the pan. (You may need to flour your hands so the crust does not stick to your fingers.). Make sure the bottom crust is evenly distributed in the bottom of the pan and into the corners. Trim off the edges of the parchment so the paper is about a ½ inch over the top of the pan.
5. Bake the bottom crust for 1 minutes at 350°. Cool for 20 minutes on rack.

Pecan Bars

If you like pecan pie, you will love these yummy pecan bars! These bars were included in our sampler tray, and our customers raved about the delicious taste and texture. The cookie crust, topped with sweet pecan filling, is worth every minute it takes to prepare and bake them.

INGREDIENTS

Crust
½ cup powdered sugar
2 cups all-purpose flour
1 cup butter - cold and diced

Topping
1 ½ cups butter
¼ cup heavy cream
½ cup honey
3 ½ cups chopped pecans
½ cup dark brown sugar, packed tightly
½ cup light brown sugar, packed tightly

DIRECTIONS

1. Preheat oven to 350°.
2. Grease a 9"x13" pan with Joy bakers spray and line with parchment paper.
3. Mix sugar and flour in large bowl. By hand blend in diced butter with a pastry tool until crumbly.
4. Pack crumb crust into the bottom of the pan.
5. Bake crust for 15 minutes.

Pecan Topping

1. In a saucepan over medium heat, melt butter.
2. Add cream, honey, and brown sugar, stirring constantly until sauce comes just to a boil.
3. Remove pan from heat and stir in pecans and spread over. Hot crust.
4. Return pan to oven and bake for 20-25 minutes. Bake until topping bubbles!!!!
5. Take out of the oven and cool. While Bars are cooling, occasionally run a knife around the edge of the pan to separate caramel from pan.
6. Cool bars completely and then cut into 1 ½"x2" bars.

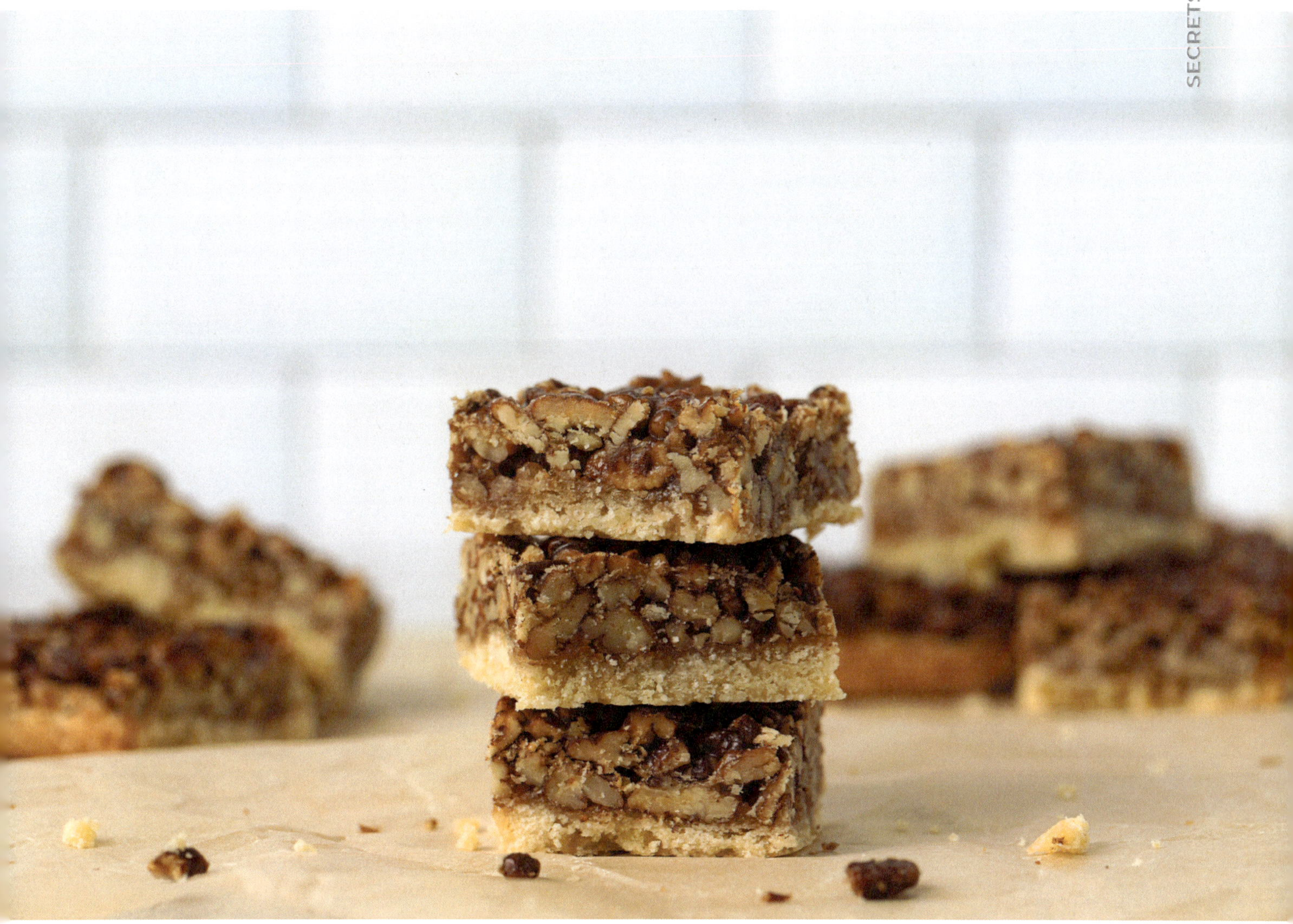

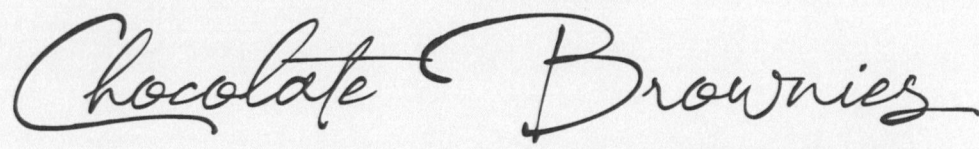

Chocolate Brownies

There is not another dessert that made my pie kitchen smell any better than baking these luscious brownies. The smell of brownies baking is intoxicating, and the taste will make your tummy smile!

INGREDIENTS

4 sticks of butter

8 eggs

4 cups of sugar

¼ tsp. Salt

1 cup flour

4 tsps. of vanilla

1 cup chopped walnuts

Wax paper

8 oz. of semi-sweet chocolate

Chips - melted slightly in microwave until softened

DIRECTIONS

1. Preheat oven to 350°.
2. Cut a 9"x13" inch rectangle of wax paper and line the bottom of pan. Also, grease the pan with Bakers Joy Spray.
3. Place chocolate chips in small glass bowl and melt in microwave for 20 seconds or until slightly softened.
4. Cream together the butter, sugar and softened chocolate chips in mixer. Mix ingredients together using a paddle.
5. Add 8 whole eggs and stir.
6. Stir in the salt and flour slowly.
7. Add vanilla and stir.
8. Add ½ cup of walnuts to batter.
9. Pour batter in a 9"x13" inch pan and top with the other ½ cup of walnuts.
10. Place brownie pan in the oven on the middle rack and bake for about 30 minutes. Turn pan in the oven every 15 minutes.
11. When brownies smell good and have pulled slightly away from the side of pan, brownies are done. Take out of oven and let cool for about 10-15 minutes. Before turning rectangle out of pan and cutting into squares.

Breakfast Breads & Coffee Cakes

Other items added to the Sweet Magnolia menu upon request were breakfast breads and coffee cakes. We sold every breakfast bread or cake made during the holidays!

There were many apartments and homes close by our Chinoe location, and many of these customers stopped by Sweet Magnolia on their way to and from the grocery store or on their way to work. They often stopped to sit in our café' and enjoy a coffee and breakfast bread or a piece of pie.

We also baked and served fresh cookies and muffins every day! My clients favorite part of stopping in was tasting the free "samples". If the customers enjoyed the free samples, we usually kept the "sweet" on the menu.

My dear friend Joe Brumette, who was also an invaluable consultant, friend, and "jack of all trades" often said that we should video our customers as they walked in during the holidays. Many clients would walk in the pie shop exhausted and stressed out from the holidays. Yet, after tasting, sampling desserts, smelling the delicious aroma of fresh pie or bread in the oven, and leaving with a homemade dessert to share at home, they would have a huge smile on their face! I enjoy thinking of how many people I met and touched in a small way during my 25 years in business.

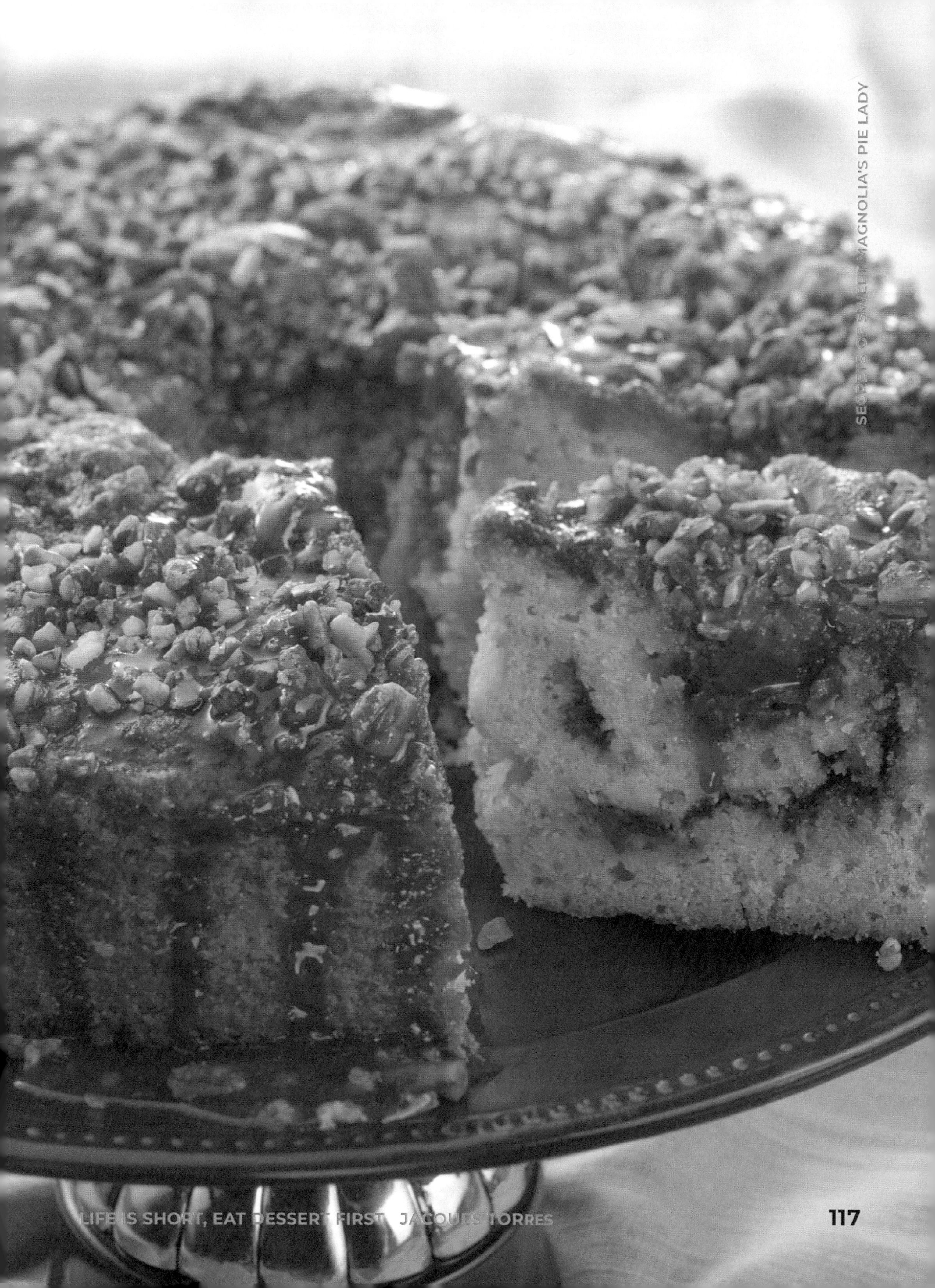

Morning Glory Muffins

MAKES 18-20 MUFFINS

INGREDIENTS

2 cups flour

1 ⅓ cups of sugar

2 tsps. of baking soda

1 ½ tsps. of cinnamon

1 tsp. of salt

2 cups of grated carrots

½ cup of raisins

½ cup of coconut

½ cup of chopped pecans

1 cup applesauce

3 large eggs

2 tsps. vanilla

1 (8 oz.) can of crushed pineapple, well drained

DIRECTIONS

1. Combine the flour, sugar, baking soda, cinnamon, and salt.
2. Then stir in the carrots, raisins, coconut, pecans, and drained crushed pineapple.
3. Make a well or hole in the center of the mixture and add 1 cup applesauce, 3 large eggs, slightly beaten, and 2 tsps. of vanilla. Mix until moist!
4. Place paper baking cups in the muffin pan holes and fill each with 1/3 cup of batter.
5. Bake for 25 minutes (set the timer for 13 minutes, check and rotate, then bake the other 12 minutes or until muffins are just done to the light touch (slightly bouncy to the touch of your finger) They may not look overly brown when they are done. Remove from pan immediately.

Sour Cream Coffee Cake

This moist breakfast cake doesn't need icing to satisfy the sweet tooth in all of us! It is perfect for the breakfast table; the dessert table; or straight off the kitchen counter as a midnight snack! When our family gathered at Nana's lake house, she would always have a sour cream coffee cake sitting out for us to enjoy! We would stand around in the kitchen, laugh and tell stories, and listen to granddaddy tell corny jokes! As we talked and laughed, the cake seemed to disappear a pinch at a time!

INGREDIENTS

2 cups of sugar

2 sticks of butter-diced

4 eggs

2 cups of sour cream

¼ cup oil

3 cups of flour

1 tsp. of baking soda

2 tsps. of baking powder

2 Tbsps. of Watkins plain vanilla

½ cup of cinnamon sugar

1 cup of pecan pieces

DIRECTIONS

1. Set our butter for 30 minutes before creaming.
2. Preheat oven to 350° and spray a 10" tube pan with Bakers Joy baking spray.
3. Combine and beat in mixer the sugar and butter on medium until fluffy.
4. Add eggs and blend.
5. Sift together the flour, baking soda and baking powder and add to creamed mixture and blend well.
6. Blend in the sour cream and oil.
7. Add vanilla and blend.
8. In a small bowl, mix the cinnamon sugar, brown sugar and pecans.
9. Sprinkle ⅓ of cinnamon mixture around the bottom of tube pan. Spoon ½ cup of the batter into a one-piece tube pan and sprinkle 1/3 of cinnamon mixture over the batter. Cover the mixture with the rest of the batter and sprinkle the rest of cinnamon mixture over it.
10. Place in the oven on a middle rack and bake for 40 minutes, then check to see if it is getting too brown. If it is already brown, cover with foil and bake for another 15-20 minutes.
11. When cake is done, remove from the oven and cool for 10 minutes before turning out on a plate.

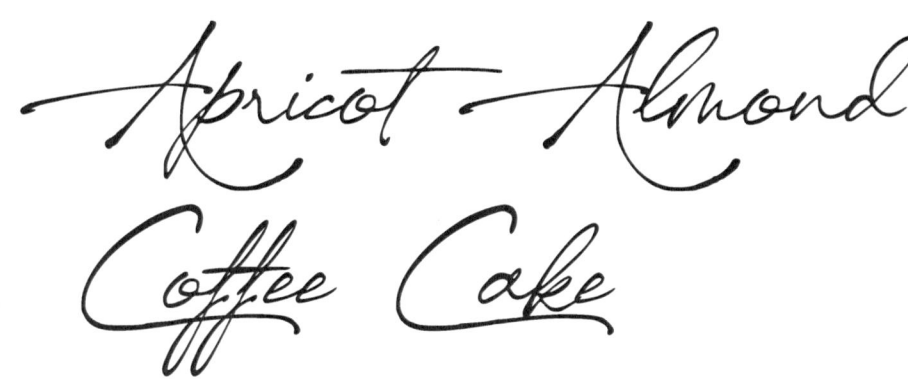

Apricot Almond Coffee Cake

INGREDIENTS

1 ½ cup butter

2 ½ cups sugar

3 large eggs

1 ½ tsps. almond extract

½ cup of apricot preserves

1 ½ tsps. baking powder

1 ¼ cup sour cream

¼ cup slivered almonds

2 ½ cups Hudson's all-purpose flour

DIRECTIONS

1. Preheat oven to 345°.
2. Grease 1 pretty bundt pan with Bakers Joy Spray. Set aside.
3. Sift the flour, baking powder and salt in a small mixing bowl. Set aside also.
4. Blend the butter in an electric mixer until creamy.
5. Add Sugar and mix well.
6. Add eggs, one at a time, blending just until the yolks disappear.
7. Blend in the almond extract and ¼ cup apricot preserves.
8. Add the flour mixture alternatively, with sour cream to the butter mixture in mixing bowl - Begin with flour and end with flour.
9. Place batter in the bundt pan and smooth evenly with spatula.
10. Bake for 55-65 minutes on middle rack in oven. Bundt is done when the top of cake springs back when pressed down with fingers. Cool for 10 minutes and then turn out onto a board or cake plate. After cake is cool, decorate top of Bundt cake with 2" stripes of more preserves (another ¼ cup) from outside cake to inside - all around the top of cake. Also sprinkle with slivered almonds over the preserve stripes. This makes a beautiful coffee cake.

Banana Foster Bread

INGREDIENTS

2 sticks of softened butter

3 cups of sugar

4 eggs

4 ½ cups mashed banana

2 ½ cups all-purpose flour

1 cup cornmeal

1 Tbsp. baking soda

1 tsp. salt

2 tsps. rum flavoring

1 cup rum

4 tsps. vanilla extract

2 Tbsps. + 1 tsp. banana flavoring

3 rounded Tbsps. caramel (bought at grocery store to make caramel apples).

2 tsps. caramel flavoring

DIRECTIONS

1. Preheat oven to 350°.
2. Spray 2 loaf pans or 4 petite loaf pans with Bakers Joy nonstick spray
3. Combine the flour, cornmeal, baking soda, and salt in a small bowl and set aside.
4. Combine the streusel topping in another small bowl and set aside: 1 cup flour, 1 cup chopped walnuts, ½ cup dark brown sugar, 1 stick melted butter).
5. Cream butter and sugar together on low in Oster mixing bowl.
6. Add 4 eggs, one at a time; beating after each addition.
7. Add mashed bananas
8. Mix all flavorings together and then add to butter mixture.
9. Add dry ingredients to batter mixture until well blended.
10. Sprinkle ¼ of dry streusel mixture in bottom of 2 loaf pans or 4 petite loaf pans.
11. Evenly pour wet batter into loaf pans and top with remaining streusel topping
12. Place on middle rack of preheated oven and bake for 40 minutes. Rotate pans and bake another 15 minutes. If bread is done, the center will bounce up slightly when touched lightly with oven mitt.
13. Let cool for 5-10 minutes before turning out of pans.
14. After removing from oven, baste top with melted butter.

Zucchini Bread

INGREDIENTS

3 cups shredded zucchini (about 3 medium)

4 cups all-purpose flour

1 cup plus 2 Tbsps. of granulated sugar, divided

½ cup chopped walnuts, TOASTED!

¼ cup packed brown sugar

5 tsps. baking powder

1 Tbsp. grated lemon rind

1 ½ tsps. ground cinnamon

½ tsp. salt

¼ tsp. ground nutmeg

1 ½ cups skim milk

6 Tbsps. vegetable oil

2 tsps. vanilla extract

2 large eggs

Bakers Joy cooking spray

Recipe makes two (8"x4") loaves of zucchini bread.

DIRECTIONS

1. Preheat oven to 350°.
2. Coat two (8"x4") loaf pans with Bakers Joy cooking spray.
3. Press moisture out of zucchini on several layers of paper towels. Cover with additional paper towels and set aside.
4. Combine the flour, 1 cup of sugar, walnuts, and next 6 ingredients in a large bowl. Then make a well or hole in the center of this mixture.
5. Combine the milk, oil, vanilla and eggs in a medium size bowl and stir with a whisk.
6. Add zucchini to wet mixture and stir well.
7. Add the wet mixture to the well in the center of the dry mixture and stir until all is moist.
8. Divide the batter evenly into the two loaf pans, and sprinkle each with 1 Tbsp. of granulated sugar.
9. Bake at 350° for 1 hour and 10 minutes or until a wooden toothpick inserted in the center of loaf comes out clean. Take out of oven when ready and cool 5 minutes in the pans on a wire rack. Cut around the outside of loaf pan to loosen bread from pan. Turn out bread from pans and cool completely on wire rack .

Bread Pudding

INGREDIENTS

⅓ cup of melted butter

24 slices (1 lb. loaf) of dry white bread

1 ½ cup of raisins

1 ¼ cup of finely chopped pecans

6 eggs - beaten

3 cups of sugar

6 cups of milk

2 tsps. of cinnamon

2 tsps. of apple pie spice

2 tsps. of vanilla

1 cup of dark brown sugar, packed

1 stick of butter

½ cup of corn syrup

½ tsp. of cinnamon

½ tsp. of nutmeg

½ cup of bourbon

DIRECTIONS

1. Grease a 9"x13" inch pan.
2. Cut the bread slices into ½" cubes.
3. Spoon ¼ to ⅓ of melted butter over the cubes.
4. Sprinkle raisins and chopped pecans over the bread cubes.
5. Combine the eggs and sugar and stir by hand.
6. Stir in milk, cinnamon, apple pie spice, and vanilla.
7. Pour milk mixture evenly over the bread cubes and bake for 40-45 minutes or until brown. While the bread pudding is cooling start making the sauce.
8. In a large saucepan, add brown sugar, butter, corn syrup, cinnamon and nutmeg. Cook on medium heat until it comes to a boil. Boil and stir I minute.
9. Add ¼ cup of bourbon to the pan and mix well.
10. Poke holes into the bread pudding. Pour the sauce over the bread pudding and allow the sauce to soak into the bread pudding before you serve it.

Yeast Rolls

The yeast rolls were always the favorite of the grandchildren. At our holiday table, Or anytime they visited, my family enjoyed the yeast rolls hot out of the oven, covered in real butter and strawberry jam. This was often a preferred dessert!

We sold every roll we made!

Sweet Magnolia sold thousands of rolls during the thanksgiving and Christmas holiday seasons. We started baking these rolls in early October to prepare for the huge holiday demand. We also delivered dozens of rolls to customers out of town for their holiday tables.

I began making these yeast rolls at the pie shop after getting reacquainted with Mrs. Louise Barton at my daughter, Michelle's wedding. I had met Louise the first time at a garden club on Rainbow Road in 1963. At the time, I lived with my husband Mike and two young girls, Marla and Michelle. As it turned out, Louise became a dear friend of my son-in-laws mother, Joyce Barnette. Joyce told me that Louise loved to make yeast rolls! Then, at my daughter Michelle's wedding reception, in March of 1987, I asked Louise if she would like to come and make rolls in my shop! She thought that sounded like fun, and agreed to try it. Louise baked rolls at the pie shop for 6 months. She and her sisters would come to the shop and make dough, pinch rolls, giggle and laugh all morning long! We would make dozens and dozens of rolls, place them on the very top shelves all around the pie kitchen to rise, and then bake them off very carefully to a perfect light brown. There is nothing like the smell of 75-100 fresh rolls baking in the oven!

Yeast Rolls

MAKES 5 DOZEN ROLLS

These were the best rolls that you could buy anywhere because they were made by hand from beginning to the end with TLC. After I sold my business and retired, I no longer had a proofer where the rolls could rise. I lit both fireplaces and placed the rolls by the warm fireplace. Now, we call these rolls, "Mimi's Fireside Rolls".

INGREDIENTS

43 oz. water
16 oz. Sweetex or solid Crisco
6 eggs
⅓ cup dry active yeast
5 lb. bag Hudson Cream flour
2 ½ cups sugar
3 tsp. salt
1 pound of butter – diced in small cubes and placed back in refrigerator until ready to use.

DIRECTIONS

1. Using large metal mixing bowl, add Crisco to the bowl. Using hand mixer, add hot tap water to Crisco and stir with hand mixer. Add eggs and blend. Add salt and sugar and continue to mix.

2. Add hot tap water to deep small mixing bowl. Slowly sprinkle yeast into water, whisking rapidly. Add dissolved yeast to other liquid in first bowl.

3. Add flour to mixture, a portion at a time, and blend. Then knead with your hand to blend further.

4. Cover tightly with Saran Wrap and refrigerate for at least 24 hours. However, do not leave in refrigerator more than two days.

5. Turn out on well floured board and knead gently to form dough.

6. Move dough to a clean well floured surface and sprinkle a little flour on top before rolling out. Roll dough our to ½ inch thick and cut into biscuits with a 2 ½ ' floured biscuit cutter.

7. Spray pan lightly with Bakers Joy and dust the pan lightly with flour.

8. Preheat oven to 330°.

9. Place one butter cube in center of biscuit and twist up and pinch to forming a ball. Dip in flour and place upside down in a 10" greased and floured pie tin.

10. Bake at 330° for 11-15 minutes or to golden brown. Check after 11 minutes. If they are browning unevenly, rotate the pan.

Sweet Magnolia Biscuits

While we were living in Savannah, Georgia in 1968 one of my girlfriends shared this delicious recipe with me. She called these biscuits "Alabama Biscuits! These yeast biscuits/rolls are thinner or "southern style.

INGREDIENTS

5 cups flour
1 tsp. baking soda
2 tsps. of salt
½ cup of sugar
½ cup Crisco shortening
2 cups buttermilk
2 Tbsps. of active yeast
2 sticks of butter

DIRECTIONS

Before beginning the process, measure and check amounts of all ingredients.

1. Sift together the flour, baking soda, salt and sugar in a large bowl.
2. Cut in Crisco with a hand pastry blender.
3. Warm 2 cups of buttermilk in a saucepan on medium heat, stirring gradually with a hand whip, just until it starts to steam. Remove pan from heat.
4. Stir in 2 T yeast and stir gradually with hand whip until yeast is dissolved.
5. Make a hole in the center of the flour and add buttermilk/yeast mixture. Mix well until flour is all wet. Using your hands, squeeze dough together tightly until it forms a ball.
6. Lightly flour your counter or board and place dough on counter. Wash and dry your hands and flour them lightly. Pat top of dough ball and sides to get any air out of dough. Continue to knead and pat until you get a firm soft ball.
7. Flour your counter or board again well and roll out your dough to ½" thick. Turn dough over and dust lightly with flour so dough doesn't stick to counter.
8. Using a 2" wide biscuit cutter or glass, cut your biscuit layers. Keep cuts close together on rolled dough. Keep gathering into a ball and rolling out until you have used all your dough.
9. Melt 1 stick of butter to soft stage in a microwave or saucepan (not until it gets separated and greasy) Add ¼ tsp. salt to butter.
10. Butter your cookie sheet and place each biscuits on pan. Keep biscuits 2" away from the edge of pan to prevent burning. Coat each ½ inch thick biscuit with butter and then top each biscuit with another layer of biscuits to make two-layer stacks. Top each stack with more melted soft butter..
11. Place cookie sheet with biscuits in the warmest place in your kitchen (away from drafts) and allow the biscuits to double in size. (about 30 minutes)
12. Bake biscuits for 20 minutes at 375° or until barely golden brown. Take out of oven and brush tops with more melted soft butter. (Add ¼ tsp. salt to melted butter if you need to use another stick of butter)
13. Recipe makes 2 ½ dozen double stacked 2" biscuits.

A FEW EXTRA
Special Recipes

There were some lunch recipes that customers requested or I thought needed to be added to our café' menu after we moved to the much larger Chinoe Creek Location.

My best friend from Paintsville, Jean Doyle, bought into my business several months after we moved to Chinoe Drive. Jean and I were best friends from first grade until our senior year. I helped her relocate down the street from me and we remain dear friends.

Jean suggested that we add her chicken salad recipe to the menu when she began working. SO WE DID! The chicken salad was a huge success! We had some customers who visited our shoppe just to purchase our chicken salad.

My oldest grandchildren, Don Penn and Ashley, did not live in Lexington so they especially enjoyed the chicken salad when visiting. When Ashley was in college at U.K., I delivered pies and chicken salad to her friends in her dorm and the Theta sorority house at her request quite often!

Other items that we added at our customers request was Southwestern Vegetable Soup and Chili. This chicken soup is very easy, delicious, and wonderful put into disposable 1 quart plastic containers and frozen to enjoy all winter long! When my family visited, they were always spoiled with soup, chicken salad, brownie bars, pie, or any other dessert they wanted!

Ashley's Favorite Southwestern Chicken Soup

INGREDIENTS

1 whole roasted chicken: remove white meat, shred and set aside.

1 (28 oz.) box of chicken broth and 16 ounces of water

1 cup chopped celery

1 cup chopped onion

2 cloves minced fresh garlic

4 cans diced tomatoes with green chilies, undrained (or substitute 2 cans of diced tomatoes for a less spicy chili!)

1 can carrots, drained

1 can corn

1 package frozen Cajun vegetables

6 cubes chicken bouillon

2 tsp. white pepper , or to taste

2 Tbsp. salt, plus.

7 Tbsps. oregano

1 tsp. basil or one hand full of chopped fresh basil

Optional: 1 can allen cut green beans.

DIRECTIONS

1. Place celery, onion, garlic, and chicken leg bones in soup pot and cover with chicken broth and water to cover ingredients. Simmer for 30 minutes.

2. Add pepper, salt, oregano, basil, tomatoes with green chilies, carrots and frozen Cajun vegetables. Bring soup to boil, then turn down heat and simmer on medium low for about 30 minutes.

3. Remove chicken legs from soup pot and add juice from roasted chicken package. Add shredded white meat and bouillon cubes. Add more water if needed. Bring soup to boil and turn down to medium low and simmer for just a few more minutes until bouillon cubes are dissolved. Stir and taste soup. Add more salt if needed to taste. Serve or freeze.

4. This recipe makes a huge pot of soup. It also freezes beautifully in small 28 ounce Tupperware containers. Reheat in small amounts. The soup should not be reheated more than once. Also do not allow the soup to sit on the stove or out of refrigerator at room temperature.

LIFE IS SHORT, EAT DESSERT FIRST   JACQUES TORRES

Chili for a Crowd

INGREDIENTS

4 pounds of ground beef - browned and drained

2-3 large onions, chopped

2 cups chopped green pepper

4 (28 oz.) cans of diced tomatoes

4 (15.5 oz.) cans mild chili beans
(do not drain beans)

Also can substitute 2 cans of great northern beans for 2 cans of chili beans

2 (46 oz.) cans of tomato juice added slowly to reach consistency that you prefer

1 Box Carroll Shelby's Chili Spice Mix
(or 3-4 Tablespoons of chili powder to taste)

1 Tbsp. plus 1 ½ tsps. salt (or to taste)

Parsley to taste

2 tsps. garlic powder

2 tsps. cumin seed

DIRECTIONS

1. Brown onion, meat, and peppers together in a very large stock pot. Drain meat mixture.
2. Add all seasonings and remaining ingredients to pot.
3. Take 3 cups of chili and put in vita mixer and puree'. Return to chili pot.
4. Cook chili on med low for 30 minutes. Serve in bowls with cooked macaroni or spaghetti if desired. Top with grated cheddar cheese.

Chicken Breast La Fayette

INGREDIENTS

4 skinless, boneless chicken breasts

¼ cup oil

1 ½ cup diced celery

1 (4 oz.) can of mushroom pieces or slices, drained (optional)

1 can cream of chicken soup

½ cup half and half cream

½ cup sour cream

1 cup mayonnaise

½ tsp. salt

1 cup grated sharp cheddar cheese

1 ½ cup crushed potato chips

DIRECTIONS

1. Preheat oven to 350°.
2. Wash and pound chicken breasts. Saute' chicken breasts in a skillet about 5 minutes on each side. Take chicken breasts out of skillet and cool. Add celery to skillet and saute'. Drain celery on a paper towel. Cut chicken in large bite size pieces.
3. Place soup, cream, sour cream, mayonnaise, and salt in a mixing bowl and stir well.
4. Stir in the diced celery and mushrooms into the mixture.
5. Place chicken pieces in a 9"x13" casserole and pour mixture over the chicken.
6. Sprinkle casserole with cheese and bake at 350° for 40 minutes.
7. Take casserole out of oven and sprinkle with crushed potato chips and bake an additional 10 minutes or until just golden brown.

French Puffs

INGREDIENTS

⅓ cup soft Crisco shortening

½ cup sugar

1 egg, slightly beaten

1 ½ cup sifted flour

½ tsp. salt

1 ½ tsps. baking powder

¼ tsp. nutmeg

½ cup of milk

DIRECTIONS

1. Preheat oven to 350°.
2. Grease a muffin pan or spray with Bakers Joy baking spray.
3. Sift the dry ingredients together: flour, salt, baking powder, and nutmeg.
4. Mix together the shortening, sugar and beaten egg.
5. Stir in the dry ingredients alternately with ½ cup of milk.
6. Pour wet mixture into muffin tins and bake for 20- 25 minutes, or until top of muffins are lightly browned and bounce up when touched with a finger.

Mimi's Double-Crust Chicken Pot Pie

INGREDIENTS

½ cup butter

2 medium leeks, sliced

½ cup all-purpose flour

1 (14.5 oz.) can chicken broth

3 cups chopped cooked chicken

1 ½ cups frozen cubed hash brown potatoes with peppers and onions

1 cup matchstick carrots

½ cup chopped fresh flat-leaf parsley

½ tsp. salt

½ tsp. freshly ground pepper

1 (17.3 oz.) package frozen puff pastry sheets, thawed

1 large egg

DIRECTIONS

1. Preheat oven to 375°.
2. Melt Butter in a large skillet over medium heat. Add leeks and sauté 3 minutes. Sprinkle with flour, cook, stirring constantly, 3 minutes.
3. Whisk in chicken broth, bring to boil stirring constantly. Remove from heat.
4. Stir in chicken and next 5 ingredients.
5. Roll each pastry sheet into a 12"x10" rectangle on a lightly floured surface. Fit 1 sheet into a 9" deep dish pie plate. Spoon chicken mixture into pastry. Place remaining pastry sheet over filling in opposite direction of bottom sheet. Fold edges under and press with tines of a fork; sealing to bottom crust. Whisk together egg and 1 Tbsp water and brush over top of pie. Bake at 375° on lower oven rack 55 to 60 minutes or until browned. Let stand 15 minutes before serving.

Dee Dee's Holiday Custard

INGREDIENTS

½ cup sugar

1 quart milk

1 Tbsp. flour

Pinch of salt

3 egg yolks, lightly beaten and strained

½ tsp. vanilla

½ tsp. nutmeg

6 marshmallows

DIRECTIONS

1. Heat milk in a double boiler or a medium pan immersed in a larger pan with water.
2. Add salt, sugar, and flour.
3. Add some slightly warmed milk to strained egg yolks.
4. Add egg mixture to double boiler.
5. Stir egg and milk mixture until thickened. Remove from heat.
6. Add marshmallows and stir until melted in.
7. Add vanilla and nutmeg and stir well.
8. Pour mixture into a pitcher and store in refrigerator until ready to serve.

Donuts for Dad

INGREDIENTS

1 (11 oz.) can buttermilk biscuits

1 quart vegetable oil

1 cup sugar

1 Tbsp. ground cinnamon

Fry Daddy appliance or large Dutch oven

Chocolate Glaze (Optional)

¼ cup half and half

1 cup semi-sweet chocolate morsels

½ cup powdered sugar

Microwave half-and-half in a glass bowl at high 1 minute or until hot. Add chocolate morsels, stirring until smooth. Stir in powdered sugar. Yield: ¾ cup.

This recipe should only be made with Adult Supervision!!!

DIRECTIONS

1. Separate biscuits and place them on a cutting board.
2. Cut a hole in center of each biscuit with an apple corer, reserving dough balls.
3. Pour oil into a Dutch oven or fry daddy and heat to 350°. When oil is hot, drop doughnuts, in small batches, into oil and fry for 30 seconds on each side or until golden brown. Remove golden donuts with a slotted spoon and drain on paper towels. Repeat with dough balls.
4. Combine Sugar and cinnamon. Roll each donut and hole evenly in sugar mixture or dip into chocolate glaze. Yield: 10 donuts and 10 donut holes.

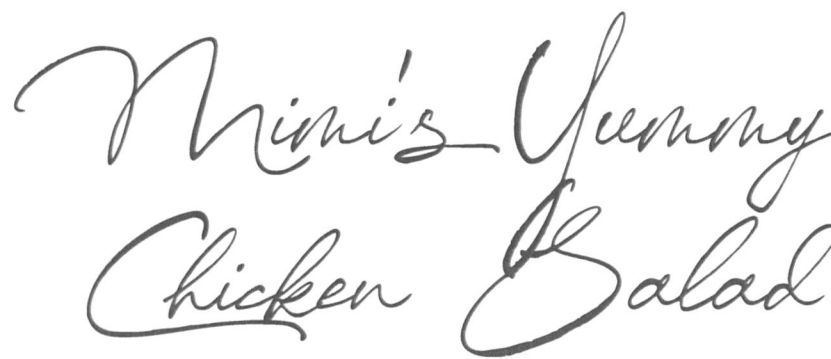

Mimi's Yummy Chicken Salad

INGREDIENTS

6-8 boneless, skinless chicken breasts
- cooked and cut up and shred.
1 small can of Swansons white premium white chunk canned chicken , drained.
1 small can of Swansons chicken, drained
2 cups mayonnaise
2-3 Tbsps. white vinegar
½ cup sugar
Salt and pepper to taste
1 cup sliced or halved red grapes
(make sure grapes are sweet)
1 cup chopped celery
1 cup chopped pecans

DIRECTIONS

1. Preheat oven to 350°.
2. Place chicken breasts in a Dutch oven with 2 inches of water and bake for 45 minutes to one hour or until tender. Take out of oven and cool to touch. Cut breasts into bite size pieces and shred some of it also.
3. Place cooked, pulled and shredded chicken in large bowl and mix well with one can of Swansons chicken. Put mayonnaise into another large bowl and add next three ingredients. Stir dressing well and add to chopped chicken mixture. Stir and fold in dressing until combined well. Add chopped celery and chopped pecans and stir well. Next, add sliced grapes and mix gently.
4. You may add more or less of the mayonnaise/sugar mixture if you prefer a dryer salad.

Crab Louis

INGREDIENTS

1 ¼ cups mayonnaise

3 Tbsps. tomato Ketchup

Tabasco or Worcestershire sauce

3 Tbsps. olive oil

1 Tbsp. wine vinegar

2 Tbsps. finely grated onion

3 Tbsps. finely chopped parsley

½ cup heavy cream, whipped

Salt, freshly ground pepper, and cayenne pepper to taste

1-3 Tbsps. chopped stuffed or ripe olives

2-3 cups cooked crab meat, flaked

4-6 large tomatoes

Lettuce and hard-boiled eggs, for garnish

DIRECTIONS

1. Blend together mayonnaise, ketchup, Tabasco sauce or Worcestershire sauce, olive oil, wine vinegar, grated onion, chopped parsley, and whipped cream. Season to taste with salt, pepper, and a dash of cayenne. Stir in chopped olives, and chill for 1 to 2 hours before serving.
2. Add flaked crab meat and stir gently.
3. Place a few lettuce leaves on each salad plate and top with a tomato half. Slice each tomato three times down the middle to form a pretty shell for the crab salad.
4. Pile crab salad on tomato halves and add sliced hard boiled eggs to garnish.

The sauce from step 1 is delicious served with any fresh cold seafood.

Mimi's Party Mix

INGREDIENTS

4 cups of corn Chex

4 cups of rice Chex

4 cups of wheat Chex

4 cups of Cheerios

4 cups of pretzels

Small can of peanuts

Small can of cashews

Medium bag of walnut halves

Medium bag of pecan Halves

1 ½ Tbsp. garlic powder

1 Tbsp. Tabasco sauce

3 sticks butter - melted in microwave

4 Tbsps. Worcestershire sauce

1 tsp. garlic salt or season salt

(your preference)

DIRECTIONS

1. Preheat oven to 250°. Melt butter in saucepan or microwave and add Worcestershire and Tabasco sauces.

2. Place cereals and nuts in large disposable aluminum roasting pan and mix together with a large spoon.

3. Pour butter mixture over the cereals and then sprinkle with garlic powder, garlic salt, or season salt to taste.

4. Place pan in oven and bake for about an hour and ½ , stirring every 15 minutes. Party mix should look golden brown not burned. Slightly add garlic salt every other 15 minutes also before you stir it.

5. Let it cool before you put it in your small containers.

Pumpkin Roll with Cream Cheese Icing

INGREDIENTS

Cake

¼ cup powdered sugar

¾ cup all-purpose flour

½ tsp. baking powder

½ tsp. baking soda

½ tsp. ground cinnamon

½ tsp. ground cloves

¼ tsp. salt

3 large eggs

1 cup granulated sugar

⅔ cup 100% Libby's Pure Pumpkin

1 cup chopped walnuts

Filling

1 (8 oz.) package cream cheese

1 cup sifted powdered sugar

6 Tbsps. softened butter or margarine

1 tsp. vanilla extract

DIRECTIONS

1. Preheat oven to 375°.
2. Grease 15"x10" jelly roll pan; line with wax paper. Grease and flour paper.
3. Sprinkle a thin, cotton kitchen towel with ¼ cup powdered sugar.
4. Combine flour, baking powder, baking soda, cinnamon, cloves, and salt in a small bowl. Beat eggs and granulated sugar in large mixing bowl. Stir in pumpkin. Stir in flour mixture gradually and mix well. Spread pumpkin cake mixture evenly onto prepared jelly roll pan. Sprinkle with nuts if desired.
5. Bake for 13-15 minutes or until cake springs back when touched. (If using a dark colored pan, begin checking for doneness at 11 minutes.). Remove from oven when done and Immediately loosen and turn cake out onto a clean kitchen towel, GENEROUSLY covered with powdered sugar! (so it will not stick to towel). CAREFULLY, peel paper off of cake. Roll up cake and towel together, STARTING WITH NARROW END! Let cool on wire rack.
6. Beat cream cheese, powdered sugar, butter, and vanilla in a small mixing bowl until smooth.
7. CAREFULLY unroll cake. Spread cream cheese mixture over cake and reroll cake. Wrap roll in plastic wrap and refrigerate at Least one hour. Sprinkle with powdered sugar before serving if desired.

Family
THE "SECRET" INGREDIENT

My team of employees rotated in the pie shop over the 25 years, but four constants remained: Nana, Grandaddy, Aunt Dede, and my daughter Michelle. These family volunteers were invaluable and very dependable. Nana and Grandaddy were the first employees to arrive in the morning and would watch over every aspect of the business if I wasn't there. Nana, Grandaddy and My Aunt Dede would pinch crusts, chop celery, cut grapes, and fold boxes for hours! They were my constant sidekicks from 8 a.m. until 11:30 every day. I saw my parents more in these 25 years than the first 17 while I grew up.

Ross and Michelle's children grew up visiting, helping, and working at the Pie Shoppe. They all stopped by often through the years just to get their favorite dessert. They had birthday parties at the shoppe and even school field trips. The kids and their friends had so much fun. When Ryan, Sarah Beth and Taylor were older they worked out front during the Thanksgiving and Christmas rush. Michelle worked at the shoppe, first with payroll and later with baking. I also sent many desserts to Lexington Christian Academy, for their school functions.

A FAMILY AFFAIR!

To the Right: Micheal, Michelle, and Marla, with "THE PIE LADY" we call Mom!
Above: Nana and Granddaddy working at the pie shop

AN ERA OF

Sweetness

Sweet Magnolia was in Chinoe Center Shopping Center off of Chinoe Drive for 19 years making a grand total of 25 years in my reign, as "the Pie lady"! To this day, I still run in to people that ask, "aren't you the pie lady?", followed by telling me how much they miss my desserts! I never get tired of hearing that!

I hope these recipes will be a blessing to you, your family, and friends as much as they have been to ours. May God Bless you all!

" *Eating is a **necessity**,*
*but cooking is an **art**.* **"**

– Gesine Lemcke

Acknowledgments

I want to thank my mother, Connie, for sharing her recipes with me so that I could "whittle down" the super-sized Sweet Magnolia recipes to home kitchen quantities. She modeled hard work, sacrifice, unconditional love, grace, and determination to me and my siblings.

Secondly, I could not have printed this cookbook without the help of my amazing husband of forty-one years. Don was my chief editor, critic, and technology expert! He shared the joy and enthusiasm for creating this cookbook from the beginning! Don is my best friend and shares our kitchen with me now since his retirement from the day-to-day operations of the car business. Surprisingly, he has become the most creative chef in our home!

Additionally, I want to thank my sister, Michelle, for her many years of helping my mom at the Pie Shoppe and compiling memories of those years through mom's story. She was also very excited about this cookbook and encouraged us along the way!

Many, many thanks to Calla and Tyler Atha who allowed us to photograph my mother Connie in their newly renovated home and redesigned kitchen by my son, Doniphan Moore.

We are grateful to my son Doniphan Moore IV who styled and executed the beautiful cover shots.

The stunning pictures of my mother on the cover were taken by the talented photographer, Kris Ellos, and the gorgeous kitchen floral designs were created by Jimmy Hensley.

Lastly, I want to also thank Melissa Bailey and Griffin Arendell at Ironside Press in Vero Beach for helping with the editing and graphic design of the original book.

IT STARTED WITH A PIE